Forgiven
A Story of Redemption

A Story of Redemption

BONNIE RAWLING

FORGIVEN
Copyright © 2018 by Bonnie Rawling

All rights reserved. Neither this publication nor any part of this publication may be reproduced or transmitted in any form or by any means, electronic or mechanical, including photocopying, recording or any information storage and retrieval system, without permission in writing from the author.

Unless otherwise marked, Scripture quotations are taken from the New King James Version®. Copyright © 1982 by Thomas Nelson. Used by permission. All rights reserved. • Scripture quotations marked NIV are taken from the Holy Bible, NEW INTERNATIONAL VERSION®. Copyright © 1973, 1978, 1984, 2011 by Biblica, Inc. All rights reserved worldwide. Used by permission. NEW INTERNATIONAL VERSION® and NIV® are registered trademarks of Biblica, Inc. Use of either trademark for the offering of goods or services requires the prior written consent of Biblica US, Inc.

Some names and identifying details have been changed to protect the privacy of individuals.

Printed in Canada

ISBN: 978-1-4866-1620-6

Word Alive Press
119 De Baets Street Winnipeg, MB R2J 3R9
www.wordalivepress.ca

Cataloguing in Publication information is can be obtained from Library and Archives Canada.

Dedication

I dedicate this book in loving memory to Peter and Marlene Tarnowski: Thank you for pouring into my life; for seeing something in me that I could not; for believing in me when I did not; and for saving my life. I can't wait to see you both again in our eternal home. Rest in peace. All my love and respect.

Dad and Mom: I'm so proud to have been raised a farmer's daughter. Thank you for teaching me independence, willpower, perseverance, tenacity, and grit. I have finally found my wings, and it's time for me to fly. Thank you both for all that you have been for me. I love you.

My girls, J, D, and R: You are beautiful on the inside and the outside. You can do anything that you put your mind to. All you have to do is believe in yourself and believe that God will guide you. There are no limits to the heights that you can fly. I'll love you forever.

Those who hope in the LORD will renew their strength. They will soar on wings like eagles; they will run and not grow weary, they will walk and not be faint. (Isaiah 40:31, NIV)

Contents

FOREWORD	ix
INTRODUCTION	xi
CHAPTER ONE—NIGHT OF TERROR: THE LIGHT COMES ON	1
CHAPTER TWO—LETTING GO	13
CHAPTER THREE—JUST STAY FOR THE RIDE	25
CHAPTER FOUR—LIL' RAGING HEART	33
CHAPTER FIVE—ANGELS AMONG US	39
CHAPTER SIX—ETERNALLY BROKEN	51
CHAPTER SEVEN—STOP THIS RIDE, I WANT OFF!	73
CHAPTER EIGHT—COWBOY…TAKE ME AWAY	79
CHAPTER NINE—FATHER'S LOVING HAND	89
CHAPTER TEN—METAMORPHOSIS…AND THE FLY	99
CHAPTER ELEVEN—SPREADING MY WINGS	107
CHAPTER TWELVE—BRIDLED	125
EPILOGUE	131
ABOUT THE AUTHOR	135
OTHER BOOKS	137

Foreword

Have you ever wondered why a sovereign, all powerful, loving God depicted in Scripture would allow His precious children to suffer injustice, humiliation, and hardship? Divine love is hard to fathom when one chooses to love others in this place called earth.

I am delighted to recommend *Forgiven* by my friend, Bonnie Rawling. Risking to love is filled with twists and turns, especially in our relationships with significant others. This book isn't just another saga of "how the world turns," but rather presents a gripping antidote to how true love can expose the essence of rich intimacy … a longing we all crave.

Bonnie takes the reader through the euphoria of victory and the agony of defeat as love is extended and encountered. Readers will experience the ups and downs of human love and recognize that when Christ's divine love shines through, our relationships can thrive.

Bonnie desires to awaken the soul to the message of divine forgiveness found ultimately through the power of God as displayed in the perfect life of Jesus. Her genuine relationship with Jesus Christ has given Bonnie the courage to endure the ride on top of the waves of hope and trust, and on the landscape of sheer abandonment.

From the first chapter to the last, Bonnie shares her story of brokenness and pain as love between trusted individuals goes awry. One initially wonders if this story will end abruptly after her many traumatic experiences. As the story continues, however, it becomes evident how God teaches her through her trials to yield her will to His and experience the depth of His love. In the events that follow, we see her desperate need to seek out His heart and be loved by Him.

We are children of the King, and our Heavenly Father shows Himself in the most unpredictable moments of life. He is free to do as He pleases, because He is good and doesn't have to explain or share His reasons. However, He has chosen to reveal Himself and His heart through Jesus Christ. He gave us His Son and Holy Spirit to demonstrate to humanity His unconditional love and desire to forgive, save, strengthen, and guide us.

Bonnie life's story demonstrates that you can look upon your problems and losses and eventually say "God is trustworthy," even when life doesn't make sense. Oh sure, one is tempted to look upon the situation and ask "Why?" But Jesus wants us to ask, "Why not?"

Read on and be inspired!

—A Pastor Friend
Harry Unger
Taber, Alberta

Introduction

There's a story in the Bible about a woman at a well (John 4:5–42). Jesus and His disciples were on their way to Galilee, and they passed by this well. Jesus stopped to rest there while His disciples went farther into town to get food. It was midday and really hot, and all of the women would have already fetched water earlier in the day before the heat of the day came. But a Samaritan woman came to the well to fetch water while Jesus was there.

Jesus was a Jew. She was a Samaritan. At that time, many Jews thought that Samaritans were unclean. Talking to a Samaritan, let alone a Samaritan woman, was not accepted at all. Also, it was somewhat peculiar that this woman came to draw her water during this time of the day, rather than early in the morning with the other women.

The fact is, this woman lived a life of shame. She had been married five times, and the man she was living with wasn't even her husband. Whether she felt too ashamed and unworthy to be around others, or she was ostracized by the other women because of the way she lived, isn't known. My guess is that it was a combination of the two, and that's why she was at the well when she thought no one else would be there.

Nevertheless, while they were at the well together, Jesus started talking to this woman. Not only did He talk to her, but He told her everything she ever did. He told her things about herself that few people could have known. But He didn't say these things in a condemning way. He did it in such a way that she felt an incredible healing touch from Him.

Jesus showed her unconditional love and acceptance, and she was so touched and healed that she went into town, proclaiming to everyone about this man she had met. Could He be the Messiah that they were waiting for? To the people who, just that very morning, she was too ashamed to be around she now boldly proclaimed that she'd had a healing encounter with this prophet! The people of Samaria were so amazed at the change in her that they went out to see for themselves this man Jesus.

***

Can we just be honest? We live in such a hurting world, a world that's craving for honesty, realness, and authenticity. Young people are hurting; adults, marriages, families, even elderly people are hurting! I believe that we're all starving for authentic relationships. When we don't find what we need in healthy, positive relationships, we look for it in unhealthy ones. I believe the cause of all of this hurt is that we've asked God to excuse Himself from our lives, our kids' lives, our schools, our society, and, in some cases, even our churches.

We want to make our own mark, make a difference, make a name for ourselves, be a good person, be the best—better than the next person—show what we're made of, and show the world we can do it on our own. Really, we just want to be our own god.

We're so busy trying to make sure that everyone thinks we have it all together—covering up our insecurities, fears, and problems with our big houses, fancy cars, diamonds on our hands, and the stuff in our lives—that we can't afford to be real.

We don't need God; He just gets in the way of our plans and our image. And besides, the stuff that He wants us to be real about is buried deep, and it would hurt way too much to bring it all up. The past is in the past, and it should just stay there. We don't want to really hear from Him anyway, because we may not like what He says!

I believe that it's time we start reclaiming what belongs to Him—our lives. It's time to get real, people. I believe we are at a crucial time in history, and we need to get real! So I am going to be completely honest with you. I'm going to get real with you.

INTRODUCTION

I'm no different than that woman at the well. Like that woman, I've been married several times—four, in fact. Whoa! Now maybe you're thinking, *What kind of person are you? I thought you were a Christian.* Maybe doubts rise in your mind about my character, my integrity ... maybe even judgments like "Who does that?" Maybe you're thinking, *I don't want to read any further.*

Well, let me tell you my story. Let me help you understand me. Let me take you on a walk of hope and forgiveness. Follow me, and allow me to take you there.

***

Before you venture into this book, I challenge you with this: I wrote this book not to preach, not to judge, and not to condemn. I wrote it simply because I believe that it is part of my life call to share my story, inspire others, give hope, and bring glory to God.

Mine is a story of brokenness, hurt, pain, anger, and a very messed-up life. It's about how God came to me in a vision, changed my life, and gave me a hope and a future (Jeremiah 29:11). It's a story of new beginnings, hope, forgiveness, and the grace of God that is only found in Jesus. But before you read on, I encourage you to think about the following.

Everyone has one, maybe two, people in their life that they really would rather not have to deal with. Maybe you don't want to see them ever again. Maybe it's someone you see every day and wish you didn't have to. It may be a family member, a co-worker, or someone at school who picks on you. Maybe it's your own mom or dad, your brother or sister. It may be a former boyfriend or girlfriend, an ex-spouse, or a former in-law. Is it someone who really hurt you? Or someone at church or at work to whom you would rather not have to stop and talk? Maybe it's just someone you think is really messed up and beyond hope or beyond reaching. Maybe that person is you. I know I have been that person for other people.

Think about that person for a minute. What do you really think of him or her? What would you like to see happen to that person? Be honest with yourself. Now set those thoughts aside for a time and come along with me on this journey.

One last note: my intentions for writing this book are to bring a message of forgiveness by sharing my story, to bring a message of hope and healing to people who have perhaps been through similar circumstances, who are in them, or who are simply looking for hope. I want to share my story honestly, authentically, and transparently without causing hurt, blame, or ill-feeling towards others; therefore, when I speak of people who are interwoven in my past, I have omitted the use of their names. As for my children, for the protection of relationships, I will refer to each of them using the first initial of their names.

It is not my intention to bring attention to anyone, to put others in a bad light, or to cause hurt. I simply want to tell my story and how God has saved such "a wretch like me." This is a story about Jesus, and He is the only one who needs attention in my story. Because of His forgiveness, I am able to forgive. Because of His love, I am able to love. Because of His grace, I am able to show grace. Because of His mercy, I have hope.[1]

---

[1] Throughout the book there are song references that correspond to that particular part of the story. These songs have been written by my husband, Bruce Rawling, specifically to complement my story ... kind of like a soundtrack to my story. Bruce's CD is also called *Forgiven*, and if you've purchased it along with this book, we suggest that as you come to each song reference, you pause and listen to the corresponding song found on the CD. I guarantee that each song will touch your heart and deepen the message.

Chapter One

NIGHT OF TERROR: THE LIGHT COMES ON

"Stop it! You're going to kill my mommy!" D screamed in horror as she and J climbed on my husband's bare back, desperately scratching him to make him loosen his grip from around my throat.

He was on the driver's side of my Sante Fe, reaching through the open back door. I was on the other side, at the open back door, where I had been trying to get R's car seat done up. He had me by the throat and was trying to shove my head under the back of the front passenger seat, and I could see my two girls peering at me over his head.

All I could do was try to keep my balance. Any attempt to loosen his grip just gave him more strength to push my head farther under the seat. Besides, it was useless. With his long, gangly, outstretched arms and his strength, there was no way I could fight back. But I knew if he managed to get me out of the way for long enough, he'd have time to get R's straps off her shoulders and get her out of her toddler seat.

I will never forget looking up over his head and seeing the terror in D's face. She could see that I couldn't breathe very well, and from the panic in her face it was clear that she really thought he was going to kill me.

The girls' scratching became even more desperate as they tried to get him off of me. He finally relented and struck back at the girls. That bought me some time to scramble up and try to get R safely buckled up.

My husband realized that I was succeeding with the toddler seat, and he charged back into the back seat of the truck. He pushed my head with such force that it threw me off balance and sent me flying backwards. I landed hard on my butt on the sidewalk. He grabbed R out of her seat and rested her on his left hip. As I desperately ran around to the other side of the SUV, I told J and D to go into the house and lock the doors.

I fought to get R out of his arms. She was crying, traumatized, and afraid. He reached out with his free arm, grabbed my waist-length hair, and used it to twist my body around until I was on my knees on the ground. Then he kicked my back with his bare foot so I crashed face first into the gravel. I picked myself up, and he grabbed my hair again, twisting it in his hand until he had me by the back of the head, and he threw me back onto the ground.

Again, I picked myself back up. This time he grabbed my right arm, twisted it, and lifted it up high above my body, forcing me to my knees. I could feel burning in my shoulder, and I heard the ripping of my ligaments, but I didn't have time to think about the pain.

He put his foot on my back and pinned me down with his weight. When I tried to get up, he pulled on my arm harder and higher and pushed down harder with his foot on my back. Then he dropped my arm and continued his attack with his bare feet, kicking me in the stomach from underneath as I tried to steady myself on my elbows and push myself up. He turned and headed across the yard, and I managed to pull myself up and catch up to him as he crossed the yard towards his truck with R still on his hip.

"You want more do ya, you b—?" Again, he grabbed my hair and used it to twist my body until I was once again at his mercy and limp on my knees. Another blow with his foot, and I was face first into the gravel. "There, that oughtta keep you down for a while, you stupid b—!"

My husband was bound and determined to leave with my youngest little girl, R. D, my eight-year-old, unafraid of his state, came to me and desperately shovelled through all of my hair so she could see my face. "Mommy," she cried hysterically, "are you okay? Mommy? He's going to take R, Mommy! You have to get up, Mommy!"

CHAPTER ONE—NIGHT OF TERROR: THE LIGHT COMES ON

She was becoming hysterical, as she could see the progress he was making towards his truck. "Mommy, Mommy, are you okay? Mommy, you have to get up. He's going to take R. Mommy, get up! He's getting to his truck."

I could hear the terror in her voice, the fear of what was going to happen to her little sister, so I got up and ran after him again to try to stop him from leaving with my little girl.

"Oh, you still want more, you little b—? Haven't had enough yet? Well, I'll give you some more if you want it that bad!" He laughed and mocked my relentless attempts to keep him from taking my little girl. I could hear my two-year-old, R, whimpering as he held her on his left hip while he took care of me with his other arm. Once again, he went after his greatest weapon, my long hair, and used it to twist my head back, bring me to my knees, and throw me to the ground.

"Uhmf," I moaned as I felt another kick to the ribs.

As I lay there barely moving, he must've felt satisfied that I would stay down this time. "Good, now stay the f— out of my way!"

He was just a few steps from his truck. I got up out of sheer fear that if I didn't, he would run me over. He got in, started the truck, and sped off with R on his lap, spitting gravel at us.

D was now clinging to me and screaming in fear as he drove away with her little sister. She cried hysterically. "Mommy, is he going to hurt R? Mommy, he has R. Mommy, can you walk? Come in the house, Mommy. J called the police, and she's on the phone with Grandma and Grandpa. Come, Mommy, I will help you."

I dropped to my knees, sobbing and in pain, trying to gather the strength to get up. I was exhausted, I was extremely sore, but mostly I was afraid of what could happen to my little girl. He was so crazy then that anything could happen as he sped out of the long driveway and went east down the highway.

D helped me to my feet, and together we walked back to the house. J, who had been inside the locked house watching everything through a window, was at the door, waiting to unlock it. "Grandma and Grandpa will be here soon, Mommy. I talked to them the whole time until Dad left the yard with R. Grandma called the police, and I called the police like four times, but no one has come yet. I don't know why they haven't come, Mommy. I called them!"

Both girls were crying hopelessly, and so was I. D looked up at me. "Mommy, I'm scared. What if he gets in an accident with R? What if he leaves?"

I tried to be brave and reassure her. I told her it was going to be okay, not knowing myself what the outcome of the night would be. The three of us huddled together crying, trying to console each other. My body was beginning to throb, my head was in excruciating pain, and even moving my hair out of my face was painful. I was in so much pain that I could hardly bear the hugs, but I knew my little girls needed to be held.

My heart started to pound in complete fear as I heard his diesel truck coming down the driveway. I didn't know what he would do now. Was he coming back for his gun? I got up, looked both of the girls in the eyes, and said very firmly, "No matter what, you girls *do not* unlock this door! No matter what! Do you understand me!? No matter what he says or does, you do not unlock it! Even if he comes to the door crying and tries to convince you to open it, you *do not* let him in! Do you both understand me? He may be coming for his gun! No matter what you see happening outside, you *do not* come out of this house, and you *do not* unlock this door!" Firmly, I said, "Do you both understand me?"

I waited for a response so I knew that they knew how important it was that they listen to me. I could tell that they were both very afraid, but I didn't have time to console either of them. I had to get out of the house before he had a chance to get up the back steps.

I went out the door and paused, peering through the window until I knew that J had locked the door behind me. I went down the back steps as he was stepping out of his truck. I tried to go around to the other side to get R out of the back. He laughed at me and said, "Do you think I'm that f—ing stupid that I wouldn't lock the f—ing doors?"

I tried to talk to R through the window to tell her it was okay. She was now sitting in her car seat in the back seat, crying. He still had his driver door open, and he peeked his head inside the door and said to

CHAPTER ONE—NIGHT OF TERROR: THE LIGHT COMES ON

R in his mocking voice, "See, R, that's what happens to Mommy when she doesn't listen to Daddy. She gets herself beat up. See, R, isn't she a stupid b—?"

R kept crying, looking over at me as I tried to calm her through the window. He left the truck running, slammed the driver door, and went up the steps two at a time to the back door. "Open the door, girls," he demanded. "Come on, D. Open the door. Dad just needs to get some clothes. Let me in." He pleaded with them as he stood there in nothing but his underwear on that cold September evening. They stayed away from the door. He tried to persuade D again to come and let him in. I could hear J telling D to get away from the door. "Just ignore him, D. Remember what Mom said."

He realized his efforts would be unsuccessful, so he started cussing at me, something about brainwashing my kids, as he walked around the house to find another way in. I started to follow him because I was afraid that he would find a way in. Partway around the house, I decided I didn't want to get caught by myself with him at the front of the house where no one could see what was happening, so I went back to the truck to try to get to my baby.

When I put my face up close to the tinted window, I could see that R was still strapped in her toddler seat, crying and afraid. How could a two-year-old little mind process what she was witnessing? She was scared, and I couldn't reach her, so I just kept talking to her over the hum of his diesel truck, trying to calm her down. "It's okay, sweetie. It's all going to be okay, honey. Mommy will get you as soon as I can. Okay, honey. Mommy loves you."

As I tried to reassure her, my husband came up the side of the house. I could tell by the way he was throwing himself into every step that he was even more angry now because he couldn't get in. He yelled at me, grabbed me by the hair again, and threw me down head first into the railway tie that lined the driveway. My head hit hard, and I wasn't sure I was going to be able to get up from this one. "Tell those f—ing kids of yours to let me in the f—ing house!"

He ran up the back steps again and pounded on the back door with both fists, yelling at the girls. "Let me in the f—ing house! I just want to get some clothes; let me in! This is my f—ing house! Let me in!" The girls stuck to the plan and stayed away from the door.

I managed to pick myself up from the ground and was again trying to calm R. She was crying even more hysterically when I heard a car turn into the driveway. *Oh my God, thank God, someone to help me!* I thought.

Careful not to alert him, I took a few steps backward to look around the side of the house to see who was coming down the long driveway. A police cruiser slowly and cautiously made its way down the lane. I kept talking to R, hoping they would pull up and see him in his rage at the back door, but he heard the vehicle pull up and came down the steps, cussing me as he walked past to see who was there.

The police pulled up, and both officers got out of the vehicle. They asked me if I had called for an officer, and I said my daughter had been calling. My husband puffed out his chest, put on the firmest and most reasonable voice that he could muster, and pleaded with the officer to reason with me and tell the kids to let him in the house.

Standing there in his bare feet and nothing but his underwear, he was making it sound like I was the irrational one who wouldn't let her poor husband in the house to simply get some clothes. "All I want is to get some clothes, and she told the kids not to let me in the house." He pleaded with the officers like he was somehow the victim in all of this.

They asked him what the disturbance was, and he said there was nothing wrong other than that he needed to get in the house and get some clothes. I interrupted and asked the officer to let my baby out of the truck so I could take her in the house. The officer got the keys from my husband and unlocked the truck so that I could get R out. She was still crying and looked cautiously around to see who these people in uniforms were and what was happening. I crawled up into the back of the big rodeo truck and calmed R with my voice as I tried to unhook all of her seat buckles with my trembling hands. As I pulled her out and held her close to me, she clung to me and nestled her head into my neck with her thumb in her mouth; tears running down her face, she whimpered and rested her quivering body next to mine. One of the officers took my husband to the police cruiser, and the other escorted R and me to the door, where the girls were waiting until it was safe to unlock. The officer asked me to get some clothes for him and told me that they would be questioning him in the cruiser and then would come in to talk to me.

The officers took a while to question him, and in the meantime my parents showed up. They had started the two-hour drive almost immediately after J first phoned them. One of the officers then came in to question me about the events of the evening. By that time, I had settled both D and R into my bed, while Mom and Dad were with J in the living room.

My head was pounding, my scalp and hair hurt, my body hurt, I was still visibly shaking, and I was in a state of shock from everything that had taken place over the past three hours. The last thing I felt like doing was sitting down and trying to explain to an officer everything that had just happened. I just wanted to lie down and make it all go away. I tried to wrap my brain around what had happened and how it all started.

As I explained to the officer, my husband had been to a roping jackpot that day, which usually meant he'd have a few beers. He was late getting home because he had stopped at the neighbours' to drop off horses, which usually meant a few more beers.

When he got home, I was in bed because I had classes the next day for my advanced care paramedic course. But I wasn't asleep, because I was worried about him drinking and driving while he had D, our eight-year-old daughter, with him. When he crawled into bed, I lay there for a long time trying to decide if I should say anything or just let it go.

Finally, I decided I couldn't let it go, because I was really angry that he was drinking and driving with D again. As I lay there with my back to him, I calmly yet with resentment in my voice said, "I don't want to fight with you about this again, but I'm just going to say that if you ever kill one of my kids because you've been drinking and driving with them, I will never forgive you."

I waited about five minutes with bated breath, and he didn't say anything, so I thought, *Okay, good*. I took a deep breath to relax and closed my eyes to go to sleep. The next thing I knew, he had my waist-length hair in his hands. He lifted me right up off the bed and said,

"You self-righteous f—ing b—! Don't you tell me what to do and what not to do with our kids!" He threw me towards the wall, and I landed where the floor and wall met. He swore at me and told me to keep my mouth shut.

I explained to the officer, "I got dressed and went and sat in the living room for a while, wondering what I should do. I didn't feel safe going back to bed with him, and all the kids were sleeping."

I told the officer how I tried to reason in my head what I should do. "Surely if I crawled into bed with one of the kids, she would wonder what had happened, but I could hear him in the bedroom still mumbling to himself and cursing me, and that's when I decided that I needed to get out of there and give him some time to cool off."

I also had to decide where I would go. What would I say if I showed up at someone's house all shaken up with three crying kids? I had talked to a friend of ours a few days before about our fighting, how his anger was getting worse all the time and how cruel he could be. She was the only one I had ever told, the only one who had any inkling as to what was happening in our home. And so I had decided that her home was the only place I could go, and that I would go there for the night.

I continued explaining to the officer. "I sat quietly in the living room for what seemed like forever because I was trying to let him fall asleep. Then quietly I tried to gather my purse and a few things. I snuck downstairs with the older girls' shoes and woke them up. They asked if we had had another fight, and I quietly explained where we were going and that we were just going to leave for the night until Dad cooled down. I told them to be very quiet. I got them to the top of the steps and told them to wait until I picked R up out of her crib."

The officer was taking notes, and he encouraged me to keep going. I continued, "I went through the kitchen and snuck down past our bedroom door to the end of the hallway. I picked R up out of her crib without her making a peep and carried her to the door. As I was slipping my shoes on, he came bounding out of the bedroom, shouting, 'What the f— do you think you're doing, you stupid b—?' It startled me and R, who jumped in my arms and started crying. It scared the heck out of J and D.

CHAPTER ONE—NIGHT OF TERROR: THE LIGHT COMES ON

"I explained to my husband that I was just going for the night, to give him a chance to calm down, and that I would be home with the kids in the morning. He tried to grab R out of my arms, and he shouted, pointing at J and D, 'You can f—ing take those two, but you're not taking my R.' Then the battle was on."

I continued my statement and did my best to remember the sequence of events, but so much of it was a blur. "I told the girls to go and get in the Santa Fe as I struggled to get out the door with R. He was trying to hold me back and grab her out of my arms at the same time, but I managed to wiggle my way out of the door, get down the back steps, and get R into her car seat. As I was trying to get her buckle done up, he came in the other side, where D was in the back seat, and pushed my hands out of the way so I couldn't get R buckled in. He kept hitting me in the head, pulling my hair, and pushing me back ... anything he could do to keep me from reaching the buckle, while he tried to take her out of the seat.

"D scrambled out of her seat and somehow got around him and out of the truck. I kept fighting my way back in and tried to push his hands away from unstrapping her. By this time, both J and D were on his side of the truck, behind him, screaming in terror and trying to get him out of the truck and away from the car seat. He grabbed me by the throat and pushed me backwards down to the floor of the truck, violently shaking me and yelling at me, like he was trying to shove my head under the back of the front passenger seat. By this time, both the girls were on his bare back, scratching him, trying to get him off."

I was crying as I recalled our nightmare. I said to the officer, "I remember looking up at D over his shoulders, and she could see over him that he had me by the throat. I'll never forget the terror in her voice as she screamed, 'Stop it! You're going to kill my mommy!' He was relentless and kept squeezing my throat harder, yelling at me and trying to shove my head farther under the seat."

I paused to get some control over my emotions and let the officer catch up on his notes. When he was ready, he asked if I was ready to go on. Through my sobs, I explained that after some time of fighting in the back seat, he had been successful in getting R out of her seat and had her perched upon his hip.

I explained how I tried to get her away from him and how he was relentless in using my hair to twist my body into a limp pile on the ground and then kicking me in the stomach or the head so I couldn't get up. "I can't honestly tell you how many times he picked me up that way and threw me to the ground, but each time I was slower and slower to get up."

I went on to explain as best I could remember. "While all this was happening, J had gone to the house like I told her to, but D didn't go. I vaguely remember D's screams of terror each time he twisted my body around by my hair. Each time he threw me to the ground D was hysterical. She would come to my head, frantically move the hair to uncover my face, and ask if I was okay. I told her to go on into the house, and she said, 'No, I'm not leaving you, Mommy. He's going to kill you!'

"Too exhausted to argue with her, I picked myself up and went after R again. Eventually I realized that he was trying to make his way to his truck, so I tried to back him closer to the house each time that I reached for R. I don't know for how long he threw my body around our yard like I was a rag doll, but I do know that I was exhausted and could tell that I was losing the battle."

I continued explaining to the officer that I hadn't known until later that J had been on the phone with my parents as they were travelling. My mom repeatedly instructed J to hang up and try calling 911 again. They couldn't understand why no one was responding. J spent the entire time alternating between 911 calls and calling my parents back so they'd know what was happening. The officer said they'd been on a rural call on the other side of town and couldn't possibly have responded any sooner than they had. He assured J that she had done the right thing, but it was just one of those unfortunate nights where there were only two officers on call in our small Saskatchewan town, and those two officers were otherwise occupied.

As I sat at the kitchen table with the officer, I realized something as I heard myself telling my story—that it really was as bad as it seemed. My parents hadn't known anything about the things that were happening in our home. I hadn't wanted them to know; I didn't want anyone to know. In fact, a large part of me didn't want to believe that I was living this way. A large part of me wanted to just keep pushing through. If I could just be a better wife, a better cook, a better rider, a better roper, and maybe, just maybe, if I was better, if I did things right, just once in a while, I would get his approval, and it would make things better. I just needed to be strong, hold my head high, keep smiling, and keep working. Then no one would know … not even me. Yet in that very moment I realized that I had become what I feared the most—an abused woman in denial—one who thinks maybe she's just going crazy, that it's just all her fault because she can never do it good enough or get it right. An abused woman … again.

> Yet in that very moment I realized that I had become what I feared the most—an abused woman in denial—one who thinks maybe she's just going crazy, that it's just all her fault because she can never do it good enough or get it right. An abused woman … again.

The officer was very patient and kind as he explained the next step that he and his partner would be taking. They would take my husband with them and question him further. We could rest easy that night because my husband would not be coming back until the morning. He said that they would have to review the matter, and they would be in touch with us as to what would come of the horrific events of that night. He advised me to see my doctor so that everything was documented, just in case we had to go to court, and to take pictures of bruising that showed up on my body and the places on my head where clumps of hair had been pulled out.

None of us really rested well that night. I lay in bed with my kids, eyes wide open, tears often streaming down my cheeks, reliving everything that had happened over and over again in my head. My parents stayed with us for a few days afterwards, and my mom insisted that I go to the doctor the next morning. I didn't want to go. It's extremely humbling when you live in a small town and work full time at the hospital, and no one knows what really happens in your home. Everyone in town was sure to know if I went in. But my mom insisted, so I went.

The doctor was very discreet, as was the nurse who attended to me. I knew both of them very well. As a primary care paramedic, I had worked alongside both of them in the emergency room, yet they upheld my integrity through the whole examination process and were very empathetic, gentle, patient, and understanding. I was very thankful that that particular RN was on duty that day.

After the physical examination, I explained what had happened, and the nurse documented it. Then the doctor asked everyone, including my mom, to leave the room. He sat on his little stool in front of the stretcher that I was sitting on, looked me in the eye, and said, "Bonnie, if you don't leave him this time, he could kill you the next time."

I looked away with tears streaming down my face, the words hitting right at the centre of my gut. I wondered if he'd known all along. I looked back at him, and no words came, only tears, but I nodded and he knew we had an understanding. The light finally went on! I had needed someone who was looking from the outside in to confirm for me that this really was my reality and that he saw it too.

Those words still echo in my mind to this day. His words, I believe, are what gave me the determination, strength, and courage to leave. I leaned on those words every time thoughts of going back crept in, every time doubts in my ability or strength to do this on my own tried to penetrate the tough outer shell I had to wear. His words were God's gift to me, I believe, to empower me to do what I needed to do.

Chapter Two

LETTING GO

I'm a country woman through and through, and being on the ranch with my husband and family meant that I was finally living my dream. At home, I was a cowboy's wife, a gardener, a seamstress, a homemaker, a very amateur roper, and a rodeo mom. The thought of having to let go of that lifestyle was very likely what kept me there for so long. I loved my huge vegetable garden and my herb garden; I loved to cook, can, and preserve; I loved to ride with the freedom of loping across an open field on the back of a horse that I trusted. I loved working with cattle, branding time, and rodeo. I loved watching my kids learn to ride and rope and barrel race, and I loved raising my girls to appreciate the simple things in life. Walking away from all of that would probably be one of the most difficult things I would ever do.

Besides all that, what would happen to the friendships we'd built in this small, rural town? I'd likely be walking away from many friends whom I cherished dearly. People would feel torn as to where their loyalties should lie. You see, my husband was born and raised a cowboy and considered himself the local "go-to man" when it came to any horse or cattle questions or problems, including breaking a horse.

He was a pasture man, calf roper, team roper, and horse trainer. He was a strong man. In fact, he's the only man I've ever seen kill a bull with his own two hands. I certainly wouldn't say he was the horse whisperer type, but people loved to bring their horses to him. We'd sat around the round pen on more than one occasion, watching him break a horse in and kill it. He would either ride it so hard that it suffered injury and became lame, or its spirit was broken. Sometimes a horse he was breakin' in would just drop dead, or it would break its own back from fighting hobbles during ground work. But I guess it's all in a day's work … right? Anyhow, none of that seemed to matter to people. It didn't seem to bother others like it bothered me. The fact was, he was the go-to man, and after I left, people would certainly have more use for him than for me; that was a given. Nevertheless, sometimes you just have to learn how to walk away.

I didn't realize until months after I left him that the freedom from being in a violent home, under constant criticism, constantly walking on eggshells, and making sure that I didn't voice my opinion too loudly—actually, the freedom from being consistently deeply sad and angry—would far outweigh the benefits of living my dream. I would also realize as I found other ways to fulfill my love for riding and horses that literally breaking a horse to death isn't breaking a horse at all. It's not the real cowboy way at all, and it's not just bad luck. And breaking a woman the same way is just as wrong.

Nevertheless, it took me five long years of fighting and of putting my kids through things that they never should've had to see or deal with to finally have the guts to say "enough." Five years of feeling like I was going crazy, like I was the one who was to blame for all the fighting, like I deserved to be shoved into the wall, pushed down the stairs, or thrown out of the house naked because, after all, I was the one who had been married before and divorced, so it obviously wasn't anything he was doing wrong.

For five years I tried to cover up what was really happening in our home because I couldn't stand to have anyone know or to face the truth myself that I had made another terrible mistake out of my desperate need to be loved. Why didn't I leave earlier? I can't explain, and it's hard to understand unless you have walked this walk yourself. Partly it was shame and partly because I wanted so badly for there to be a different ending.

CHAPTER TWO—LETTING GO

After that night of terror, my parents stayed with me and the girls for a few days because we were all too shaken up to be left alone. And quite frankly, no one had any clue about where we should all go from there. My dad talked to my husband the next day, after he got home from wherever the police had taken him, and he agreed that he needed to give the girls and me some space because we were all in shock. He moved out to the RV that was parked in the yard. He said he was sorry for what happened that night, and he wanted badly to make up for it.

I thought he really was sorry. He cried each time he saw the girls in the window from across the yard where he was working. I could see him working out at the barn, and he hung his head all day. He came to the house at night in tears to say goodnight to the girls. And as terrified as they were, they wanted to see him too. It was a really tough week.

Admittedly, his tears were making it difficult for me to decide whether to leave or not. I really loved him. I really loved this ranch. And I really loved our life. Seeing him like that all week played on my heartstrings. At the same time, the words of my doctor echoed in my mind as I wrestled with pain and confusion, wanting to make the right decision for my kids.

In the days to follow, the RCMP ended up laying assault charges on my husband. He would now answer to more than just me about his anger issues. I wasn't sure if this was a good thing or a bad thing. If I stayed, it would be like a constant burr in his saddle blanket, and he was sure to blame me for it. *What will come of that?* I wondered as I pondered our future.

That week I also contemplated this new thing called faith that had been nudging at my heart. Up until now, I had ignored it, or at least kept it hidden, perhaps because I knew in my heart it would be too precious a thing to share with my husband. But now, as I wrestled with so many things, I wondered what God would say about what I should do with my life.

***

Rodeo was something we did almost every weekend as a family, and the rodeo finals were coming up that very weekend. D had worked hard all season to make the finals in pee-wee barrels. How could I ask her to miss that? My dad talked to my husband, and he agreed that he would take D's horse for her. He would stay at his parents' for the weekend, I would stay at my parents' lake house with the kids, and we would meet at each of the rodeo finals performances ("perfs") so that D could finish her barrel-racing year. After that we would have to figure things out. We decided it was best just to get through the weekend of the finals first.

It was pretty nerve-racking being there. We followed a rodeo circuit where everyone knew everyone, and by that time most people knew that something had happened between us. I tried my best sitting in the stands to not show my physical pain or my emotional pain and to be strong for the girls.

I didn't know how his parents would be, so I wasn't really sure how to act when I first saw them. I was sure they would be pretty quiet, knowing what their son had done, and I thought for sure they would keep their distance until the weekend was over.

My parents and I decided that it would be easier to leave R at the lake with my mom rather than take her to the rodeo perfs with us. First, she was only two and wouldn't really miss it anyway. Second, she would have been way too overtired, and none of us could emotionally handle an overtired toddler at that time. Third, I was too physically sore to be chasing after her at the rodeo. Finally, we weren't sure how my husband's parents would be with the girls, and I couldn't handle any more emotional stress right then. We sure called that one right!

I was sitting in the stands when I heard my dad and my husband arguing behind the stands. He was demanding that my dad bring all the girls to the rodeo the next day because they would be going to stay with him and his parents. I looked around the stands; it was quite obvious that I wasn't the only one who could hear their raised voices!

As the arguing got louder, they gained almost more spectators than the barrel-racing event that was happening in the arena. It wasn't long before I heard my father-in-law join in. I decided to stay out of this one—until I heard my mother-in-law join in. I wasn't able to move without a lot of pain, so I hobbled my way down the stands through the crowd and behind the stands to see what all the arguing was about.

My father-in-law said to my dad, "How can you stand there and support that stupid b—ch?"

My dad said to my husband, "Obviously, your parents haven't been clued in to what has gone on here, son."

My mother-in-law piped up, "Oh, we know exactly what has gone on! Your daughter is a little b—ch! Beating on my son that way!"

My dad, not believing what he was hearing, laughed. "Her beating him up? Ha!" Looking at my husband, Dad said, "Are you going to stand there and let them believe that load of sh—?"

My mother-in-law grabbed Dad's forearm and shook it to get his attention. "Oh, I saw the scratches on his back from her," she exclaimed at the top of her voice.

Finally, I'd had enough. I threw her hand off my dad's arm and yelled back, "Those scratches on his back are from my girls trying to get him off of me because they thought he was going to kill me!"

The shouting went back and forth for some time before my dad finally said to my husband, "So is this how it's going to be? You're actually going to be that kind of a man who lets your parents believe that your wife beat you up?"

His answer was all I needed to make up my mind. My husband puffed out his chest, and with as firm and reasonable a voice as he could muster, he said, "Well, that's what happened."

On the way home to the lake that night, all I could do was stare out the window as we drove in silence. I couldn't believe what had happened. I couldn't understand what had changed from just that morning when my parents and I left the ranch with the kids, and my husband left in tears for his parents' home. *How could he just lie like that? How did this whole thing get completely turned on me?*

I was deeply confused, but I knew that it was over. I knew that nothing would ever be the same and that all hope was lost. I knew that I had to get out, I had to get out right away, and it wasn't going to be pretty.

I lay in bed that night overwhelmed with thoughts. The hurtful words of my husband and his parents penetrated my very core. So many things to sort through, so many decisions. *What am I to do? When am I to leave? How am I to leave? Where am I to go? Is this actually happening? Is it actually over?*

Not knowing where else to turn, I prayed. "Oh God, help me, God. What am I to do? Help me, please." I prayed as I cried myself to sleep.

In the morning, I woke early. It seemed as if God Himself had answered all my questions while I slept. It was like He had all the answers lined up, and He was just waiting for me to ask for His help! I just had to keep strong and allow Him to lead.

I awoke that morning with a determination and strength that came only by divine providence—I am sure of it. I knew I had to get out that very weekend. He was away, and it would be the only safe time to go. I was determined, and I knew this would be the only way. But how could this be possible? It was early Saturday morning, and he would be home from the rodeo finals on Sunday night. Besides, I had to be at the rodeo with D for the Saturday night perf and the Sunday afternoon perf, and I wasn't about to let her be alone with him or his parents right then with all that was going on!

My parents tried to reason with me and get me to think through the realities. They knew how exhausted I was and how impossible a task it would be. After all, it was Saturday morning, and everything would have to be done by Sunday afternoon!

I insisted that it had to be that way. I just knew in my heart what I needed to do. I called a friend and told her what had happened at the rodeo the night before. I told her that I needed to get out … fast. And I told her my plans to do it that very weekend. She told me I was crazy.

About half an hour later, she phoned back and told me about a house in a new subdivision in town that had been for sale, but had sat empty for almost two years. She said maybe if I phoned the owners and explained the situation they would let me rent it. I tracked down the owners, whom I had known before they moved away, and explained that I had to be out that weekend and why. With hardly even a hesitation at the other end, the answer was a resounding, "Yes!"

Okay, next problem. How would I move all my stuff? It had only been three weeks since our new RTM home had been moved onto the ranch, and we had moved everything from the old ranch house. The thought of leaving our brand new home was heartbreaking to me, but there was no time for that nonsense. I called everywhere that I could think of within a 200 kilometre radius to find a moving truck. No luck. My final attempt was one more business in the area where my parents lived. On the other end of the phone, the woman was empathetic with my desperation for a truck, but she explained, "I'm terribly sorry, but the only truck I have available is only available today and tomorrow."

"Perfect!" I exclaimed. "That's all I need it for!"

She seemed confused, but I was ecstatic! About an hour and a half after my initial phone call to my friend, I called her back and said, "We're on our way with a moving truck, and we're moving into our new house!"

"What? That's crazy!" she exclaimed.

"Do you think you could get a few people to help us move?" I asked.

"Oh, don't you worry about the people. You bring the truck; I'll bring the people," she said confidently.

My brother drove the moving truck, J rode in the truck with her uncle, and Dad and I took separate vehicles to make the two-hour trip. As I drove, I calculated in my head when I would have to leave in order to be back in time for D's rodeo that night. I couldn't miss it! She needed me there, and I couldn't let my husband know that anything was up, or things would be very ugly! I had to be back and play it cool at the rodeo.

When we arrived at our home on the ranch, it was just the four of us—my dad, my brother, J, and myself. It was just so overwhelming! So much to pack—all of those things that I had just spent the last three weeks unpacking into our new home and finding a special place for. I was overwhelmed, coming to grips with the fact that my marriage really was over, and on top of it, I was too physically sore to lift even the smallest box.

My dad, my brother, and J started packing boxes. All I could do was wander around the house crying, saying goodbye to our family's hopes and dreams, taking newly hung family pictures off the wall, picking up special things that we had collected or been given over the years, and storing up special memories in my heart. The pain in my heart and in my broken spirit was even more intense than the physical pain in my body from the night of terror that had happened less than a week before.

I was standing in the kitchen, feeling quite overwhelmed and discouraged at the thought of the task before us, when through the front window I saw an amazing sight that broke the waterworks, and my sobbing turned to deep weeping. Down the driveway, a half-ton truck slowly and steadily made its way towards the house. The back of the truck was so loaded with young men that fitting in another body wouldn't have been possible! It was my friend's family along with almost the entire high school football team and their coach!

I stood on the back steps as they pulled up to the house, too full of emotion to even speak. My friend climbed the back steps and held my trembling body while I wept on her shoulder. "Sorry we're late," she said. "I was at your new house cleaning, and I lost track of the time. I got the keys from the real estate agent, and we've been there all day, getting it ready for you."

Then, seeing the chaos with all these new bodies who were looking for something to do, she took charge immediately. "Does everything go?" she asked me.

I answered, "No. Whatever was his before we got married stays."

She said, "Okay, you tell us what goes, and we'll load it!"

In three and a half hours, our entire house was packed, loaded, taken into town, *and* unloaded into our new house! It's amazing what God can accomplish when we allow Him to lead! It was clear to all of us that this truly was His divine providence and His leading.

It was getting on 4:30, and I knew I had to leave so we could make the 7:00 perf. My brother and J stayed to finish cleaning out the odds and ends from the ranch and get things organized at our new house. My dad and I drove back in separate vehicles to my hometown, where the finals were being held.

After the evening perf, Dad took D home with him, and I drove the two hours back to our new home. I needed to be there bright and early in the morning to finish getting the rest of the odds and ends from the ranch house and to say my final goodbyes.

The next morning, I went out to the ranch on my own for the last time. As I meandered around our home and our yard, I thought of all the hours that we spent out there in that arena, riding and roping as a family. I walked slowly around each corner of our ranch. I would always remember how the kids used to play on the stack of bales, the treehouse that the kids used to play in, my garden—oh, how I would miss my garden! Oh, the time, effort, and love that I had poured into it! I would miss those corrals at branding time, seeing my husband out the kitchen window working at the barn or in the shop, our beautiful yard, the horses—how I loved these horses, how I loved watching them lope into the yard together when my husband would stand at the barn calling to jingle them in in the morning—all of our cows, the dogs, even the cats. All of it. I was saying goodbye to it all. Broken hopes and dreams.

Purely exhausted, I drove slowly down the long laneway, taking every last memory and picture in that I could. I knew it would very possibly be the last time I ever made that drive. Physically, my body, scalp, and muscles were still extremely sore from being thrown around like a rag doll, and I was exhausted from all the driving, moving, crying, and lack of sleep. Emotionally, I was exhausted from all the trauma, grief, loss, and heartache of our lives being torn apart. And mentally, I was exhausted from all the questions and decisions: How did this happen? Why is he lying to his parents? What happened to all the tears and how sorry he was? What am I to do? Where are we to live? How are we to move? What needs to be packed? What needs to be left behind? Where do the boxes all go?

Over those two days it did seem that I had God's favour. So much had been accomplished in two days that it was nothing short of a miracle. Now it was Sunday just before noon, and I needed to get back to my hometown for D's Sunday afternoon rodeo perf. The moving truck needed to be back early that afternoon, so my brother drove it back while I drove back with J. We talked about all that had been accomplished in the past few days. In an attempt to make it not hurt so much, we focused on all the victories that we had experienced just in the last two days.

We made it back in time for D's rodeo and waited with bated breath until she finished her last run. Then we all headed back to the lake together. I was proud of D for racing under such stress and fear to even be in the same vicinity as her dad. Mind you, my dad didn't let her too far out of his sight at any given time!

On Sunday evening, my lawyer said that under no circumstances was I to leave my parents' house until he got a court order in place stating that the girls were to remain in my custody until my husband answered in court to the charges the RCMP had placed on him. I needed the rest anyhow, so I didn't argue.

By mid-week we had the court order in place, and we were able to head back to our new home! D and R didn't know what to expect. We had kept them sheltered from a lot of what had happened the past weekend so as not to cause more stress than necessary. R was too young to really process things anyhow, and D—well, it was time to start explaining where Mommy and J were all weekend. J and I were just relieved that we had a safe place to be going "home" to.

As I drove, I wondered what had happened when he got home from the rodeo and discovered that I had left. *Sure would've liked to have been a fly on the wall in that house when he walked in and realized I was gone!* I thought. Part of my heart broke for all the broken dreams. Part of me wished it could be different. Part of my heart broke for the pain that he would've felt when he walked in and realized that I had left. Part of me hated him for all the hurt he was causing and the lies he was telling, and part of me couldn't afford to even go there, because I had three girls who needed me to be strong. It was time to let go.

The weeks went by, and I was finally strong enough to go back to work. The girls and I were settling into our new home and our new life, learning to walk in the ways of the Lord, and learning a whole new way of life.

It did seem that we had the Lord's favour in everything that we did, and I began to learn the most important lesson He could teach me—that not all lessons are easy. Often it's through the most chaotic and difficult things we face that He shows His sovereignty.

> It did seem that we had the Lord's favour in everything that we did, and I began to learn the most important lesson He could teach me—that not all lessons are easy.

Not long after we moved in and were settled, the house that had sat on the market for two years without even so much as a viewing all of a sudden sparked the interest of a new young couple who were moving to town. They say that you should never make any big decisions when you're in turmoil, and buying a house was certainly *not* something I wanted to do at this point in my life. But their offer to purchase forced my hand.

The people who owned the house told me that they would give me first crack at buying it, because they knew the trauma that the girls and I had just been through, and they knew that the last thing we needed right then was more.

Ironically, the woman who had to approve my mortgage application was the same woman who just put an offer on the house in which we were living! Through this circumstance and our Bible study together, we ended up becoming really great Christian friends!

As God would have it—which definitely wasn't the way that I would've done it (and I thought He should know that)—I became a new homeowner. I spent the winter painting my girls' bedrooms specially for each of their personalities, painting the living room and the rest of the house with my own colour choices, painting Scripture verses on the walls, and decorating the house just the way I liked it.

God blessed me with good friends, and I discovered that being a single mom of three girls was a heck of a lot easier than being in a violent marriage with three girls. I also began to learn some of the most valuable lessons of all. Sometimes you just have to let go and let God.

Chapter Three

JUST STAY ON FOR THE RIDE

Fall turned to winter, winter turned to spring, and I was really starting to get my feet under me. There were many trials, but we managed to make it. I spent my time making our house a home and doing my best to get myself and my three girls through the crisis of a broken family. As a result of the night from hell that marked the end of my marriage, there was seldom a night without my girls experiencing night terrors or bad dreams. The two youngest became permanent additions to my bed each night.

In addition to walking my children through the brokenness, I had, by this time, managed to secure myself the maintenance/ambulance "blend" position at the hospital as well. This allowed our health region to have a full-time ambulance staff available at the hospital as well as a full-time head of maintenance. And I was it. I worked full-time daytime hours at the hospital on maintenance, and if my radio went off, I dropped everything I was doing and ran for the ambulance bay. Unfortunately, this arrangement also meant that I was often the one "on call" 24/7 for both jobs as well. The way I saw it, I was just doing what I had to do to survive for my girls. Between J, who was fourteen, close friends, and neighbours, my kids were providentially always taken care of when I literally had to run out the door on an ambulance call or to fix a broken line on the old steam boiler.

With spring in season, it was also the time to get moving on the ranch—only I wasn't on the ranch anymore. This brought a whole new set of emotional trials that I would have to walk through. The grief for the loss of family hopes and dreams came like a wave again, as quickly as spring itself had sprung. There's an old saying: "You can take the girl out of the country, but you can't take the country out of the girl." An old cowboy friend who had taken us girls under his wing needed help moving horses, and I couldn't resist the chance to get out and ride.

I could afford to take a few hours off work to give him a hand. After all, it would only be a quick trip to get there, saddle up, move the herd, and get back to work. One of my co-workers agreed to cover my call while I was out of radio service for a few hours.

A few days later, as I lay in my hospital bed, I found myself staring at the patterns on the ceiling, trying to piece together the events of the previous days. Flashes of horses' hooves were so vivid that I was forced to close my eyes as I thought through what had gone wrong.

I let my mind go back to the beginning of that day. I remembered leaving the yard on that big grey stallion with all three of my girls standing at a safe distance, waving to me as we brought the herd through the yard. The old cowboy led as lead horse, and I was bringing up the rear of the herd. We made our way through the yard and down the long laneway, hoping that no one was coming down the perpendicular dirt road as the herd picked up speed. They moved nicely across the road and through the first gate.

The old cowboy, still leading, took a sharp right and headed through the second gate into the holding pasture. The move was going really smoothly, just as it should have, when suddenly the last half of the herd headed east down the dirt road on a real runaway! *What the heck happened?* I thought. *No time to think—I've got to stop those horses!* There was no time to panic, only to kick it into high gear. We had twenty-five horses on the run! I kicked that big grey stallion up. "C'mon, boy, we gotta get ahead of those horses … they're gonna be gone!"

We moved into high gear. The horses were on the run along the dirt road, and we ran like the wind down low in the ditch, passing one horse after another. With each long stride that big grey stallion loped

CHAPTER THREE—JUST STAY FOR THE RIDE

his way up the side of the herd, getting to the front of the pack in no time at all!

We leaped up from the ditch onto the road, and the herd slowed enough to allow me to turn them around. I gave a quick glance back down the road, hoping to see the old cowboy waiting on the road about a mile back, and sure enough there he was, sitting in the middle of the road, waiting on me to get them turned around. *Ready or not,* I thought as I brought up the rear of the runaways, *here we come.*

The old cowboy timed it just right, and the herd followed him beautifully into the first gate again. Then he made that sharp right again into the second gate. I was just bringing the last of the herd through the first gate when it happened again—half the herd in a scramble and on the run again! *What the ...? How?* I thought. Then I saw the dog. *The stupid dog cut 'em off!* It all made sense in that split second, but there was no time for scolding him.

The old cowboy looked back just in time to see me race past him, again bringing up the rear of a herd of runaways. This time they were headed across the stubble field—well, at least they were off the road! He yelled as I rode past, "What the ...?"

I yelled back, "The dog! Send the dog back to the yard!"

Once again I kicked into high gear. "Okay, Grey, here we go again." I cheered him on, knowing this would be a cinch for him. "Okay, let 'er go, boy," I said as I hunkered down into the saddle. He knew exactly what he had to do.

In the thirty seconds it took for that stallion to once again get ahead of the herd, it felt like absolute freedom. What a rush! Loping at that incredible speed with each powerful stride underneath me, racing alongside the herd, I felt heart-pounding adrenalin and like we were one. No other horse I had ever ridden had that much power!

I got the stallion positioned just right. As we approached the front of the herd to get them turned around, the herd slowed and allowed us to move into a right turn. "C'mon, boy, nice and steady. Let's get these girls turned around!" I said as we entered the turn.

One stride into the corner, two strides, and then the slightest slip in the mud of his front left leg. "Oh, no! Don't go down on me, boy—

ahhhhh!" The ground was just wet enough from the rain the night before that the slightest wrong move would've caused a slip.

He didn't go down, but it was enough of a stumble at the speed we were going to throw me out of balance with him. I was squeezing with all I had to keep my legs in that saddle, all of my weight on the left stirrup, trying to fight my way back in the saddle. On my way off the left side of the saddle, I reached with my right arm for the saddle horn with all I could—stretched—couldn't reach it. *Oh, this is gonna hurt!* Smack!

I came down hard off that big stallion, flat on my back. I'd had so much weight on my left leg that my boot had gone right through the left stirrup, and if that big stallion wasn't on the run before, he sure was now!

In a matter of seconds, I was on the ground, and my helpless, motionless body was being bounced and dragged beside those long strides. I remember coming to and feeling my body being pulverized against the dirt and rocks, and my head and body being tossed around like a rag doll as the long strides of the big stallion thundered beside me. I hoped and prayed that somehow the big stallion would know that I wasn't safe and would stop. *Please stop*, I thought. Suddenly, my foot dropped out of the stirrup, and my body came to a sudden stop. *Oh, thank God.*

I was in and out of consciousness. I don't know how long I lay there, probably only seconds, before I heard the thundering of hooves coming. *Oh no, he's taken lead horse*, I thought. Everything went black.

"Bonnie ... Bonnie, can you hear me? Bonnie, honey, don't move. We're going to put you on the spine board. Bonnie, it's very important that you don't move. Come on, honey! Can you squeeze my finger and let me know if you can hear me? Come on, Bonnie, can you hear me?" I could hear the worried desperation in the voices that I knew so well. I knew they were my ambulance partners, and I knew how worried they were—I could hear it in their voices. I tried to let them know that I could hear them, but I just couldn't respond. I heard bits here and there of their conversation, but I couldn't really put it all together. I just knew it was bad.

The next thing I remember is the excruciating pain in the back of my head. The hardness of the spine board was almost too much for me

CHAPTER THREE—JUST STAY FOR THE RIDE

to bear. I heard the familiar voice of the X-ray tech to whom I usually brought the patients, only this time it was me on the board.

The pain—in my back, in my pelvis, and especially on the back of my head—was unbearable. I remember trying to be coherent, trying to talk, trying to make sense of things in my head. I remember bits and pieces of the two-hour ambulance ride into the city and the throbbing on the back of my head, the nausea, the dizziness, the spinning, the headache. I even remember thinking, *Next time I have a spinal going into the city, I'm going to be a lot more sympathetic with them, because I'll know exactly how they're feeling!*

At the hospital in the city, the series of tests, X-rays, and CT scans seemed to take a lifetime. I was in and out and don't really remember all of what happened, but I do recall overhearing the ER doctor in his confusion ask my EMS partners, "Okay, tell me the story again?"

My partner said, "She went down off the horse, her foot was caught in the stirrup, and she was dragged about half a mile and then trampled by fifteen or twenty horses."

I remember the doctor saying, "I can't believe there's nothing! There's no way I'm letting her off that spine board until I know for sure. Do everything again. I need to know for sure!" Then, what seemed like an eternity later, I heard, "Are you absolutely sure that there are *no* fractures—no nothing? Are you sure?"

The consulting doctor reassured him. "Yes, we've done it all twice. There's nothing."

A long pause. "Okay, let her off the board. Man, that is one lucky young lady! I've never seen anything like it. That's one tough girl!"

I don't remember much of the two-hour trip in the ambulance back to our local hospital, just that without that spine board under me, the padded stretcher felt like heaven! Now as I lay there trying to make pictures out of the patterns on the ceiling of my hospital room, my thoughts wandered again. Well, more than that … I started having a conversation with God. I was pretty new at talking to Him, but after my experiences the previous year when God first started nudging me and revealing Himself to me, and after our "new house" miracle, I now knew for sure that He was listening, and somehow I knew that none of this was happening without His notice or consent. I prayed, "God, I don't really understand what You're teaching me here, but thank You so much that I am still here. Thank You, God. Thank You."

My thoughts wandered back through the amazing things God had done in my life since that horrible night of terror with my ex-husband—the healing in my heart, the peace in our home, a new start. *Okay, God, You've got my attention now. What are You doing with me? How is a horse wreck that almost killed me possibly part of Your plan for me? How am I going to work and support my girls now? I don't think my thirty-four-year-old body can take much more trauma! What's all this for, God? What's all this for?*

"What the heck are you trying to do, girl? Get yourself killed? You know we're already short staffed on the ambulance, and now you're out of commission—again!" My favourite co-worker kidded me as she walked into my room in her scrubs. She'd had her share of life's hard knocks, which she covered up with a mean bark, but her bite wouldn't hurt a flea, and I was thankful that she had a soft spot for me.

She was actually one of the few on the ambulance crew with whom I could really talk and trust. She was one of the few who had really been there for me in the months after I left my husband. In a small town, not many people want to take a stand for what's right. It seems that it's better to mind your own business and talk behind people's backs. But she was one of the few who could see a spade as a spade, and she wasn't afraid to say it!

She was also the old cowboy's wife. She sat down on the edge of my bed, and I asked how he was doing. She said he was taking it pretty bad. "He was pretty worried about you. He thought you were dead when he rode up to you in the middle of that stubble field. And he rode like crazy to the yard to call the ambulance, even though he didn't know if he should leave you in the field with those horses or not. Now that things look like they're going to be okay for you, he's doing better. But," she said, "he was just sick, Bonnie. He was just sick. Especially knowing that the girls were back in the yard waiting for you guys to come back. He didn't know what to say to them. He just knew he had to call and get back to you."

She seemed to lose herself in the thought of what could've happened that day. "Anyhow, enough about that; you just worry about getting better and getting back to work with me! What am I supposed to do without you at work? It's just no fun without you!"

I replied, "I'll tell you one thing. The next spinal that we take to the city is getting a ton of sympathy from me! Wow—being on that spine board for six hours is enough to kill anyone!"

As she got up and headed back to the rest of her patients, I stared out the window across the lawn of the hospital property, a lawn that needed mowing, but with me lying there, that responsibility would have to fall on the shoulders of my maintenance co-worker.

Once again, I found myself getting lost in the thoughts of just how lucky I was to be alive that day. I wondered if my ex-husband had heard what happened and if he was glad that everything was okay, or quietly wishing that things had gone really badly. *Jerk*, I thought. *I can hear him now, laughing with his cowboy buddies about me comin' off that big grey stud, and saying how he would've been too much horse for me anyway.* Oh well. That part of my life was over, and I didn't have to worry about what he thought anymore.

The little footsteps coming down the hall brought me back to what was real. I could hear giggles from R and D as they raced down the hospital hallway, trying to be the first into my room. The excitement of seeing my girls was just what I needed at that moment. As D squealed while rounding the corner into my room, I shushed her so as to not disturb the other patients in the hospital. She giggled her mischievous little laugh and proudly announced, "I beat you, R!"

R wasn't far behind with her little footsteps, and retorted in her three-year-old voice, "No faiw, D—you cheated!"

J, trying to hush both of her little sisters, came in, telling the girls in her responsible tone of voice to stop running in the hospital. She was followed by Grandpa, who had been by himself with the girls at the house since the accident because Grandma was away.

D tried to hop on the bed, but any movement of it was too much for my tender body, and J quickly corrected her. R wanted to snuggle, so I told her that if she was really careful she could come and sit beside me.

I was so stiff and sore from my head down to my toes, I felt like I had been hit by a truck! But all that mattered in the world to me was right there around my hospital bed, and as I lay back to take it all in, I knew that they were all I needed on this earth.

I'm not sure if it was on that day in the hospital room or in the months to follow that I realized that God used that horse wreck as a pivotal moment in my faith life with Him to begin the metamorphic phase of becoming His, to change me completely. Through it I would come to realize that everything in my life up to that point had been allowed by Him. Even though I had made tons of really crappy choices and desperately tried over and over to screw up my life, He was there all along!

> This was pivotal, and I knew it. Would I simply follow God's plan for my life, in faith? Would I allow Him to mould and shape my tenacious character, unbreakable spirit, and intense passion for His purposes?

There I was, in a hospital bed where I was of no use to anyone but Him. There I lay, with my battered and bruised body, facing some of the most difficult decisions in my life, and I was completely useless! God was asking me if I would finally yield to His will for my life. Or would He patiently have to re-teach me the lesson, because I would insist on my own way again?

This was pivotal, and I knew it. Would I simply follow God's plan for my life, in faith? Would I allow Him to mould and shape my tenacious character, unbreakable spirit, and intense passion for His purposes? Would I now be trusting enough, humble enough, weak enough, teachable enough, and willing enough to give Him the reins and just stay on for the ride?

Chapter Four

LIL' RAGING HEART

Half drunk and tired, I fought to keep my balance and get my shoes on in the doorway of our house. My mother was standing at the top of the steps with her hands on her hips, and my dad was standing beside her, watching me struggle with my shoes.

I was in a rage after just watching her dump my forty-ounce bottle of vodka that I had gotten for my sixteenth birthday. It was about 5:00 a.m., and I had been out all night at a dance with friends. I'm not even sure how I got home, but I was sneaking in through my brother's basement bedroom window with my bottle tucked carefully under my arm when my mom surprised me with, "What do you think you're doing?"

She grabbed my bottle and dumped it down the laundry room sink while I protested and called her names. "That's my birthday present, you f—ing b—ch!" I screamed as I fought her for my bottle as it was being glugged down the drain.

Now I was leaving. I was so tired, but I was more angry than tired. I yelled obscenities at her, slurring my words. I finally managed to get both shoes on the proper feet. I stood up, using the railing to balance, turned around, and yelled as I stumbled out the door, "I hate you!"

I stumbled down the sidewalk in front of our house. I wasn't sure where I would go in the wee hours of the morning—probably to crash at a friend's house.

***

Anger is such an intangible emotion, and I spent most of my life entangled and embittered in it. Where does anger come from? What makes people so angry that they can't function as healthy, happy, well-balanced individuals?

I've spent a good part of my life trying to answer these questions, trying to free myself from the dark hole inside that at times wells up like a roaring lion, ready to attack every living thing around me. This rage, this anger, what is it?

It's simple. Anger is hurt, deeply buried hurt, that has become hardened and calloused and can't be expressed in any other way than to rise to the surface like a volcanic eruption of unhealthy emotion.

***

Late October 1975, I was five years old and a "big girl," already in kindergarten. I loved my school, a big old brick building with character, and I loved my kindergarten teacher. I admired her waist-length brown hair and how gentle and patient she was with each of us little ones. School was so exciting for me! I was proud to be a "big girl" and able to go to school every second day.

The grade six class was having their annual haunted house and Halloween party, and I was beyond excited! I didn't know what to expect, but I knew it was a big deal, because everyone at school was talking about it. Much to my disappointment, the last day of the haunted house, and my only chance to experience it, was on a day when it wasn't my turn to go to school. I remember being devastated that I wouldn't be able to go through it, so I lied to my mom and told her I was sure it was my day for school.

On my way to school, I was hardly able to contain my excitement with the anticipation of going through the haunted house. I walked as fast as my little legs could carry me! What I didn't consider, however, was that once I got to school, I would still have to face my teacher.

Much to my dismay and heartbreak, my teacher informed me that because it was not my day for kindergarten, I would have to go home. My pleas to her were futile, so there I sat, on the big cement stairs, crying with disappointment.

CHAPTER FOUR—LIL' RAGING HEART

As the morning bell rang, streams of kids rushed up the big cement staircase, racing to get to their classrooms, excited for the day to start. My older cousin, who was in Grade 6 at the time, came to comfort me and see why I was so upset.

After I explained everything to him, he said, "Well, come with me. Let's see what we can do about it." He held my hand and, patiently waiting for me to keep up with him, led me all the way up the long flights of steps to the infamous Grade 6 hallway. It was so exciting to be up there with all the big kids! Some of the girls greeted me at the door with an excited, "Bonnie, cutie! What are you doing here?"

My cousin, glad to be the hero in the situation and have the girls' undivided attention, explained my dilemma to all the girls who had now gathered around. As they heard the story, they all chimed in with "Awwww ... you poor thing! She's such a cutie."

My cousin proceeded to plead my case with his teacher and asked if he could take me through the haunted house before I had to go home. As I stood there in the boot room of the Grade 6 classroom, I was almost breathless with suspense, hoping that this strange teacher of "big people" would have mercy on a cute little kindergarten kid. As it turned out, I was little prepared for what was to come.

We all have those moments in life that, when you look back later, you realize were life-changing, life-shaping, or life-moulding in one way or another. I remember that day when I was just five years old like it was yesterday. I remember the excitement of walking to school that morning; I remember the crushing feeling in my heart when I was told I had to go home; I remember the old-school smell of that Grade 6 classroom as I stood there in anticipation of what my fate would be. I remember the exciting yet oh-so-scary feeling when the reality set in that I was actually entering the unknown of the haunted house. I remember the slimy, gooey feeling on my little fingers as I put my hand in the bowl full of "brains." I remember feeling comforted and safe as my cousin sheltered me from behind with his arms around me as he led me in the darkness from one scary station to the next. I remember the fear and anticipation of being in the dark and not knowing what was coming next or where to go.

I also remember the panic, confusion, feelings of betrayal, and crushing feeling in my spirit when I felt my cousin's hand reach down the front of my pants into my panties and feel around my privates with his fingers. I remember that suddenly the fear of the haunted house became a small detail somewhere in the back of my mind, and my biggest fear was whether I could get away from this cousin of mine whom I had once trusted. It was dark and scary, and the panic and fear changed from excited-scared to terrified-scared. I remember the panic to get out and get away. I remember trying to wiggle away and how he pulled me close to him, whispering in my ear, "See now, you like that, don't you?"

I remember breaking free from his grasp and making my way through the darkness with my hands out in front of me as I tried to feel my way out. I saw a light and raced out of the maze. The girls were all waiting for me, excited to see how I liked it, but I raced past them to get out of the school as fast as I could. I remember my cousin calling after me and chasing me, assuring the girls that he would comfort me. I raced down the steps as fast as my little legs could go, and I remember hearing his footsteps getting closer and closer behind me. I remember him catching me halfway down the steps and whispering in my ear not to tell my mommy, because she would be really mad at me—after all, I was the one who lied to her so I could come to the haunted house. I remember once again breaking free from his grip and running until I got across the street and around the corner, out of sight of the school, where I could once again breathe. I remember crying as I walked the nine or ten blocks home from school that day, a little girl with a broken spirit. I remember that there was a change in me. I could feel it—a sadness, a brokenness that I couldn't explain. It was like I lost my childhood spirit that day.

> I remember that there was a change in me. I could feel it—a sadness, a brokenness that I couldn't explain. It was like I lost my childhood spirit that day.

***

CHAPTER FOUR—LIL' RAGING HEART

Blending families in the fifties was not an easy task, but my grandparents worked hard at it. My grandfather, widowed with five children, and my grandmother, divorced with two, were determined to bring unity into their unique family and create a peaceful home where everyone was welcomed and felt safe. As their children grew and had families of their own, that unity meant lots of family gatherings throughout the years, sharing private beaches, trips to the farm, and often bi-weekly visits to Grandma and Grandpa's house.

I remember the intoxicating smell of turkey throughout Grandma's house and the excitement as a young child of seeing all of my cousins and aunties and uncles. The entire family gathered around to eat the huge feast that Grandma had prepared. As our numbers grew each year with one or two more new cousins, we spilled over into the living room and then into the downstairs family room, because there were just too many to fit around the table. I also remember that as I grew older those family gatherings became less and less fun for me and more and more a time of fear, with roots of growing bitterness.

That day in the haunted house was the first time my cousin abused me sexually, but it certainly would not be the last. A seven-year-long game of cat and mouse began that day, a game that I never wanted to play. At family gatherings I constantly sought safety in numbers. I spent a lot of time on my grandpa's knee, the safest place to be, but when the political debates in the room grew too hot, Grandpa would shoo me away and tell me to go play with the rest of the kids.

My older female cousin was the safest one to play hide-and-seek with. She would help me find a place and get settled before going to find her own place to hide. I don't know if my cousin sat back watching and waiting for me to get hidden before making his move, but it never failed that just when I was enjoying the suspense of being in a really good hiding spot, trying not to giggle and give my place away, he would show up!

Just before the countdown was over, out of nowhere, there he was, taking his opportunity to fondle me before whoever was "it" came and found us. I grew to hate hide-and-seek. I grew to hate any games at Grandma and Grandpa's. I grew to hate family gatherings. Nowhere was safe.

Even summer holidays at the lake weren't safe. As I would walk from our cabin up the hill to Grandma and Grandpa's cabin, I was always careful to be very quiet as I passed behind my cousin's cabin, which was halfway in between. I swear he used to sit at his window and watch for me coming. It never failed—if he spotted me going by, he would lure me back to his cabin, where he would violate me again. If he couldn't lure me back, he'd take a risk right in the middle of the road and sneak a feel. Each time he violated me, he whispered in my ear, "I know you like it, and if you tell your mommy, she's going to be mad at you."

So I never told my mom, or at least not for a very long time. And I grew not only to fear him, but to hate him. I hated even the mention of his name. I didn't know how to process my feelings, and over time a small part of me deep inside became hard, cold, and bitter.

Unfortunately, over the years that small part of me would grow bigger and bigger, harder and harder, angrier and angrier. It was the source of my childhood nightmares, my childhood ulcers, and my hidden childhood pain. In time, all those confusing feelings of betrayal, hurt, fear, and anger hardened in my heart and turned into shame, anger, rebellion, and, eventually, rage.

Chapter Five

ANGELS AMONG US

By the time I was twelve years old and old enough to tell my cousin to stop, I had already begun acting out the hurt, pain, and anger that I myself didn't understand. I was well on my way to becoming one of the thousands of misunderstood hurting teens of the day. I was already smoking, drinking, and partying. At fourteen, I was drinking regularly and was heavily into the party scene.

On New Year's Eve of 1984, we were on our way to the Rocky Mountains for a family ski trip. In my opinion, I was really too cool to stay in a hotel room with my younger cousins, especially considering that my brother was allowed to bring a friend on the trip. I had raced BMX bikes with this guy and even though I was still in junior high, and he was in senior high, as well as going out with one of my friends, I admittedly had a crush on him. Somehow I managed to convince my mom that I should be allowed to stay in the "adult" room with my aunt, my brother, and his friend. The three of us teens stayed in our room for New Year's Eve while all of the adults partied in another room. I flirted with my brother's friend all night and was putting myself in a compromising situation. But my evening ended prematurely as I passed out early because I was so drunk.

I lay down on the bed to try to stop the room from spinning. It didn't. It just kept spinning, and I wished I could make it stop. I was completely unable to function, though intermittently I could hear conversation between the two boys, and at one point I heard my brother saying he was going to get more booze.

Shortly after he left, I felt a warm sensation of excitement when his friend sat on the bed next to me. I couldn't really do anything about it, but I hoped he would kiss me. He stroked my face to see if I would wake, and I moaned to let him know I could feel his touch. I hoped he would kiss me and keep gently stroking my face. I was unable to move and my body felt heavy, like a ton of bricks had fallen on the bed when I lay down.

The excitement I felt in my tummy turned to panic when I realized what was happening to me. He threw the covers off of me, pulled my legs off the bed, and lowered my body onto the floor. He was careful not to drop my head on the floor, and I could tell that he was panicked and in a hurry.

I really didn't know what he was going to do. I just knew that I couldn't defend myself, and fear grew inside. He dragged me across the floor of the hotel room into the bathroom, pushing my head and shoulders as far under the bathroom counter as he could. Then he struggled to get my legs in around the door so he could close it.

He locked it and proceeded to pull up my shirt. Then he pulled my sweatpants and panties down to my ankles. I was panicked inside, trembling with fear, but in my drunken state was unable to do anything but moan with disapproval. He struggled to get his pants down and position himself on top of me in the cramped space between the door and the toilet. Then he had his way with my semi-conscious body as I lay on the cold bathroom floor. I tried to move my legs, to close them, and he kept forcing them open.

It hurt, and I tried to tell him I didn't want this. He kept grunting with frustration because he was obviously in an awkward position and in a hurry for fear that someone would come in the room.

Without wasting any time, he quickly pulled up his pants, opened the bathroom door, checked all around, and dragged me back to my bed, feet first. I sensed the panic in him, fearful that someone would come in the room while he was trying to get me back in bed.

I was so repulsed by him that I didn't even want him to touch me. I hoped someone would walk in and catch him in the act. He dragged my dead-weight body to the side of my bed and then grabbed me under my arms, hoisted me up onto the bed, and covered me with the blankets. Then I passed out.

The next morning, I woke up with a headache and a horrible feeling like I had just had a bad dream. My aunt was beside me in the bed, and I looked over to the other bed to see my brother and his friend. I lay there, realizing that my bad dream wasn't a dream after all. I thought through what I could remember from the night before, and I just wanted to roll over and die.

I snuck out of bed, gathered all of my things from the room, and quietly went into the bathroom. I felt so violated, so filthy. Along with the feelings of betrayal and hatred, I was terrified at the thought that I could possibly be pregnant. I wasn't really even sure yet how all that worked or if it was even possible, but I was scared.

I stood in the hot shower for a long time, quietly crying deep, painful tears and trying to cleanse all of his filth from my body. I got dressed in the bathroom, shoved my stuff into my bag, and left the room, trying not to wake anyone. I wandered the hallways and the lobby of the hotel until I thought someone in the other two hotel rooms we had rented would be up. I was tormented with my own thoughts, *Why did I do that? Why did I have to stay in that room with them? Why did I have to flirt with him? Why? How could I be so stupid?* That was the first night of our ski trip, and I would have to endure the rest of the trip with this guy who had just raped me.

The very next night, I insisted that my mom allow me to stay in a hotel room with my cousins so I didn't have to be anywhere near him, but it didn't matter how far I tried to get away from him. He did everything he could to make sure things appeared normal to my family, even sitting beside me in restaurants and in the car. It felt like he was rubbing it in my face, and I was disgusted.

After the Christmas holidays, I looked forward to going back to school. I was relieved to be going back to normalcy. Finally, maybe, I could escape the trauma I had just lived through. But I wasn't prepared for what I would face in the school hallways that day.

As soon as I came through the doorway, I could feel the tension. My friends whispered to each other as I walked by, gave me dirty looks, and called me names under their breath. I was really confused. I couldn't for the life of me figure out what I had done. As if my life could get any worse than it already was!

I spent most of the morning trying to figure out who exactly was mad at me and what exactly I had done wrong. In the gym locker room, I finally asked one of my friends. She told me she thought I was a slut, and accused me of sleeping with my friend's boyfriend. When I reacted in shock and confusion, she accused me of playing dumb and said that my brother's friend had already confessed to his girlfriend that we'd slept together while we were on the ski trip.

He had told his girlfriend (my friend) that he was really sorry and wanted her to hear it from him firsthand. So not only did this guy rape me, but he also covered up for himself by saying we slept together so that everyone would think I was the slut. Everyone bought it, even my closest friends.

Walking home from school that day, I don't know that I've ever felt so empty and alone. Almost ten years after I made the lonely walk home from kindergarten, I was walking down the same long avenue to my home, feeling the same numbness, emptiness, and betrayal.

I couldn't wait to get into my room, close the door, and just cry. I was a wreck. I felt so alone, so deeply wounded, so hurt that I could physically feel the ache in my heart.

My parents were waiting for me at the kitchen table when I got home that day. My brother was pacing around the dining room angrily. *What now?* I thought. *How could this day possibly get any worse?*

My mom started talking to me about "some concerns" they had. She went on and on about how disappointed they were in me. How could I do something like sleeping with my brother's best friend? How could I possibly do something like that? "Bonnie, you are only fourteen years old …" Their voices faded in my mind as I stared out the window.

I'm not sure what they said or how long they went on. Every cell in my body was screaming out in pain. Just being in my own skin was almost too much for me. My eyes filled with tears. My heart filled with tears. My own parents actually believed that I could do something like that! Finally, after they went on and on for what seemed like forever, I screamed out, "I didn't sleep with him! He raped me! I don't know why he is telling everyone that we slept together, but he raped me!"

I went through the full account of that night in the hotel room, explaining every detail and reminding them of how my behaviour changed after that night for the rest of the ski trip, how the very next night I had asked to move into the hotel room with my younger cousins, whom I had previously thought I was too cool to stay with. How I had tried to avoid him and my brother for the rest of the trip.

My parents both sat there with horror on their faces as they listened to the nightmare that I had just gone through. It all made sense to them from the things they had observed. I could see that they were filled with regret that they had bought into the story that accused their own daughter. I could see the way they hurt for me, but it was too late. I was beyond reach now.

The next few weeks were numbing. I felt detached from my parents; in fact, I shut them out completely. It was all I could do to make it through a day at school and endure all the nasty whispers, dirty looks, and name-calling.

I became so depressed that I didn't think my life was worth living. I felt ashamed, and I didn't see any way out but to end my life.

One day I came home from school and took a razor blade from my dad's bathroom. I locked myself in my bathroom and pulled the top drawer out in front of the door so that no one could possibly get in. I sat on the floor, sobbing uncontrollably, convincing myself of all the reasons why this was the best plan. My mind was filled with dark thoughts about how everyone else's lives would be easier without me. My parents' lives would be so much less complicated without a messed-up daughter. People at school would find someone else to talk about, someone else to hate. Even my brother wouldn't have to deal with having an annoying sister.

I pressed the blade to my wrist and made a shallow cut just to see how much it would hurt when I cut deeper. Tears streamed down my face, and I could barely focus on the shallow cut line that was starting to leak blood. I sat there and watched it bleed, and I wondered how deep I would have to cut to make it bleed fast and how long I would lie there before I'd bleed to death.

As I sat there trying to muster up the courage to go through with it, suddenly I heard a voice. It wasn't loud. It was a gentle male voice. He said, "Bonnie, My child, don't do it. I have so much that I want to use you for."

The tears stopped. I looked around and tried to make sense of what had just happened. *Did I really just hear that? Did that really just happen? Was that God?*

Instantly my mind filled with thoughts of hope. I thought about my parents and how, even though things were messed up right then, I knew they really loved me. I thought about my little brother, who was the only one small enough to get up through the laundry chute to let my parents into the locked bathroom. I thought about what he'd find when he crawled up into that bathroom, if I decided to go through with it. Then thoughts about growing up, getting married, and having my own kids filled my head. I wanted to get there. I wanted to experience all of that.

I sat there for a long time as I let the tears slowly fall, slowly fade, and naturally dry up on my face. The sobs stopped and I sat there, deep in thought … in awe, actually … trying to wrap my brain around what had just happened on that bathroom floor, trying to resolve in my mind the calm, peaceful voice that I had audibly heard: "My child."

Bruce's Song: "Don't Give Up"

***

I acknowledged that I'd heard the voice of God that day on my bathroom floor; however, for many years to come, I would choose not to acknowledge the gift of life that God gave me that day, or tell anyone of it. My choice to continue to do things my own way resulted in one downward spiral after another for many years.

Ultimately, I was just a hurting kid, trying to survive in my own little world—a world where no one could reach me, a world where I

CHAPTER FIVE—ANGELS AMONG US

> Ultimately, I was just a hurting kid, trying to survive in my own little world—a world where no one could reach me, a world where I didn't want to be reached.

didn't want to be reached. Anger saturated my very core, and in my rebellion I was misunderstood much of the time. My destructive choices affected anything and anyone who was close to me. It didn't seem to matter what it was, I could mess it up—unless, of course, I was drunk or high. Then I didn't really care.

I found freedom from the pain and the heaviness of the anger when I drank or got high. The more I did that, the more I could laugh again, and the better my life was—at least that's what I thought. But the sobering up to reality when I wasn't high was difficult.

I made sure that friends surrounded me, and I was really good at fitting in with any, and all, "status" groups at school because I was such a great partier and really good at covering up my pain with a big, beautiful smile, laughter, and a carefree attitude. But in reality, it was all just a facade.

The truth is, I wasn't a good friend. I repeatedly put my friends' and other people's lives at risk by drinking and driving. I thought it was funny to make guys scream like a girl by driving in a crazy way when I was drunk. It was only by the grace of God that I didn't kill myself or someone else when I was in high school—although killing myself is what I secretly hoped for.

The truth is, boys were indispensable to me. I had a deep void inside that needed to be filled, a need to be loved. Many people, even my friends, thought I was promiscuous, but I really wasn't. I would tease guys and lead them on, but when things got to a certain point, I'd have flashbacks and shut down emotionally and physically. Most of the guys in my high school knew that I was just a player. The girls just thought I was a slut. I didn't care about either; I could drink it away on the weekend anyway.

The truth is, most of my high school classes weren't even worth my time to go to, because I couldn't absorb anything unless I was high. I scraped by, barely getting the marks to get through all of them. In fact, I'm sure that some of the teachers passed me just so they wouldn't have to put up with me for another semester!

I hated school; mostly I hated the hallways of my school. I hated the looks, the whispers, the fake friendly laughs. I hated walking down the hall on a Monday morning, not sure what had happened on the weekend or what I had done. I hated my life; I just wanted to party, get drunk and high, and make it all go away.

Many weekends the police would come knocking at our house to question me about something I had either stolen, someone I had beaten up, or worse. I had no respect for authority. Sure, I could smile really nice and use my best innocent "nice girl" voice, but as soon as I turned around, I was cussing and swearing that it was someone else's fault that I got caught. Whether it was teachers, the police, my boss, or my parents, I didn't care what any of them thought or did to me. Anger and rebellion ruled my heart.

One day in Grade 11, I was so drunk and high that I actually went to the bathroom on the front lawn of my high school, right in front of the school parking lot and classroom windows. As a result, I got kicked out of school. Though I did manage to graduate, I didn't know what I would ever do with my life that would be of any use to anyone. I was pretty sure that anything I attempted would be a complete waste of time and energy.

Apparently, I was not the only one with this low opinion of me. One time I was at a party, standing at a distance from the bonfire where people were warming themselves, when an incredible roar of laughter caught my attention. As I listened to the conversation, I heard some guys making fun of people in our grad class, and one of them was me. They jokingly named me the "most unlikely to succeed" from our graduating class, a comment that brought more roars of laughter. In my mind, I can still see a picture of the guy that said it, throwing his head back in laughter, like he's painted on my memory wall from yesterday. It was a moment that I would store up in my mind, one that would eat away at my self-esteem and self-worth for many years to come.

The worst part of my life in high school was living at home. I'm not sure how my parents, or I, survived my living at home during my teen years. I lived at home only because it was convenient for me. I did whatever I wanted, whenever I wanted. My parents' rules didn't really matter to me; they only caused the fights that were so prevalent in our home. It didn't seem to matter anyway. As long as I was out of my mom's hair, she seemed to be happy.

Often I would think back to that day on the bathroom floor, but I still wasn't ready to acknowledge that God spoke to me and saved my life that day.

***

I have found that sometimes in life when God is trying to get our attention He teaches us through difficult times and circumstances. These sometimes end up being pivotal moments, experiences that have the potential to change us forever, if we allow them to. These moments, I believe, are gifts from God. He has given me many of these gifts over my lifetime, though there are a few that stand out more than others.

On an extremely foggy January evening when I was in Grade 10, the guy I was dating was out partying with my brother. He was very inebriated and decided to leave the party to give a girl a ride home. Just minutes after he dropped her off, he was making his way along the ring road around the outskirts of the city. There was a train across the tracks, a train he couldn't see for the fog. He hit the train with such speed that the small jacked-up 4x4 truck he was driving buried itself under the train into a flat piece of metal. The cab of the truck was flattened back into the truck box, and he was killed instantly. That accident gave me a wake-up call and was the catalyst for me to stop doing drugs. I knew that if I didn't quit, my life could end like that.

I had another life-changing experience when I was in Grade 12. One of my close friends committed suicide. I knew he had hard things in his life, but I had no idea that he was struggling so much. How could I not know? Considering how much I struggled with thoughts of suicide when I wasn't drunk, how could I not have known?

His death hit me very hard, because I knew how easily it could have been me. After his death, I had a new outlook on life, a new awareness of the value that it carried, and a fresh perspective and empathy for the hurt that others carried. I believe that his death, as painful as it was for his family and for so many others, was instrumental in saving mine.

Those experiences made me decide that it was time for me to do a few things right. I quit doing drugs, and I started to make some changes for the better, changes that I knew had to happen. Though I was a long way from the end of the journey, it was a start.

Bruce's song: "Run to You"

***

In 1993, Alabama recorded a song written by Don Goodman and Becky Hobbs, titled "Angels Among Us." It's one of my favourite songs, and I do believe that sometimes God sends angels to help us along our way.

My parents decided that it was time for me to move out on my own, so they kicked me out of the house. I was finished high school, and although I was upgrading my marks, they didn't see any reason why I shouldn't get a taste of what life is really like. I needed a bit of a reality check at that point—in fact, I probably needed more than that—and I was soon to get one. I found a small basement suite and tried to be brave and make it on my own.

There was a certain gentleman, whom I saw almost every day. He must have seen something in me that I couldn't see and thought that he could perhaps reach me when no one else could. Almost daily, for weeks, he asked me the same question: Would I want to live with him and his wife, get out of my little basement suite, and focus on school?

I repeatedly declined his offer, yet in the face of my arrogant rejection, he humbly and persistently continued to ask. One day, I reached such a low that I finally walked into his office and asked if the offer was still open. That same day, I packed up my small apartment and moved into the home of my high school principal and his wife.

I lived in their home for almost a year, and although I didn't fully appreciate it then, all that they did for me, made me realize that someone saw something in me that I couldn't. It gave me hope. They were a light

CHAPTER FIVE—ANGELS AMONG US

for me, like angels on earth, to show me God's way. Their unconditional love saved my life and changed me forever.

Though I was a long way from being where I needed to be, I was a lot further along than a year before. But there was still this thing, a huge void in my being, an emptiness that I couldn't seem to fill.

So still seeking, I got engaged on my nineteenth birthday. I'd finally found someone who had the same motto in life: "Life's a party!" By late winter, however, I felt a struggle in my heart and knew that this was not what I wanted for the rest of my life. In February, I broke the engagement off and started moving on with my life.

A few short months later, I found out that I was carrying his child. Now there was a wake-up call. I had a little baby inside of me that was depending on me to have it together! This was real! In the first few days, I struggled to allow this reality to sink in. My life changed instantaneously. Everything changed. My future was not just my own anymore. Up until this moment, my life had been such a mess and I wondered how I could possibly do this.

Once I found out I was pregnant, and had absorbed that truth, I knew there were changes that I had to make. I just made up my mind that I had to do this! I quit drinking, quit smoking, and actually quit partying altogether. I honestly think this was God's way of saving my life. It wasn't just me to think about anymore. I was twenty years old when I gave birth to a beautiful baby girl! She was the most beautiful baby I'd ever seen. She was like a gift from heaven, and I thought my heart would burst with love for her.

I knew in my heart she was another little angel that God had sent to help me along my way, and I wanted to honour Him for it. I would tell no one, but I named her after that guy who, I knew in my heart, had saved my life on the bathroom floor that day, Jesus Christ.

Chapter Six

ETERNALLY BROKEN

There is something to be said for the strength that it takes to be a single mom. Although I was alone and responsible for this little one, having J in my life also gave me purpose and taught me perseverance. I knew it wasn't the ideal circumstances to be bringing a baby into the world, as a single mom, but it was what I needed to get my act together.

I just felt so privileged that God would have enough confidence in me, to give me this gift, this little child that depended solely on me, that I didn't want to screw it up in any way. I was an incredible mom. I was patient, kind, and loving. I would whisper in her ear every night that she was beautiful on the inside and out, and that she could be anything she wanted to be, if only she would believe in herself and that God would guide her always. J and I did everything together. She was such a little cutie and got smiles from people everywhere we went. She was my pride and joy!

I finished a year of university in Saskatchewan before moving to Alberta to go to school. I wanted to be brave and face the world, just the two of us, and I felt strong enough and confident enough that I could do it!

We were a great team, and we had a pretty good thing going! After a year of college studies, I found out that I'd have to wait a whole year to get into the Social Work program I wanted, so I got a job in a small town near the foothills of the Rocky Mountains. J and I were able to find a little house on an acreage where we could be near the things we loved— horses, cows, and kittens!

We had our own little garden and gathered wood for the winter. Life was treating us very well! However, I would discover something about myself during this time that would be the beginning of many more years of hard lessons learned. This void, this emptiness deep within, that I thought was filled with love from my beautiful baby girl, was still there, unsatisfied.

It would be the men that I attracted into my life at that time that would send me into a deep depression. One after another, unhealthy men would be attracted to my magnetic, yet needy, personality. I found myself trying so desperately to fill this emptiness, and all the while destroying everything good that I had built around myself. Finally, I reached rock bottom when I gave in to a guy that was pressuring me to "date" him, and he ended up weaseling thousands of dollars from me. I hit such a low that I couldn't handle life anymore—mentally or emotionally.

I recognized that I was having a breakdown, and one of the hardest things that I would ever have to do in my life was call my parents and ask them if they would take J for a few months while I tried to pull myself back together. Perhaps it was a mistake to send her away, but I thought I was doing what was best for her. I knew that these issues ran deep and I needed to get better for me and for her.

They came with the half ton truck and loaded her things, and my every reason for living drove away right before my eyes as I watched her wave with such deep sadness in her face. I lay in bed and cried for an entire day. It felt like my heart had just been ripped out of my chest. So many questions ran through my mind: What was I thinking when I assumed I could do this on my own? How could I send her away? Will she ever want to come back? Will she ever forgive me? Will I ever get it right? Why does everything I touch end up destroyed? What am I to do with my life? Is it even worth living now?

CHAPTER SIX—ETERNALLY BROKEN

***

I found a counsellor who specialized in sexual abuse cases, so I packed up my little house on the acreage and moved myself south where I could be close to my counselling sessions and treatment clinic. It was there that I started to really seek after God, to try and find some real meaning in my life.

There was a church that was distantly associated with the counselling clinic I went to, so I started going to church in the evenings. As I became more comfortable, I started spending more and more time there, attending some of their evening meetings as well.

A guy there seemed to take an interest in me, but I didn't have men on my mind. I only wanted to get well so I could get back to my little girl. Nevertheless, I observed him for a long time, and decided he was authentic. I found myself more and more intrigued with him and attracted to him as he would share his heart in our evening meetings. I loved the way he laughed at everything and seemed so easy-going and genuine.

We started going for coffee, sharing more and more of our time together, sharing our stories, our hearts, and our faith. Once I learned his full story, however, I was hooked. He had grown up on the streets of Montreal after being kicked out of the house at a very young age by his abusive mother. He basically raised himself in backyard sheds and on the streets, trying to make his way through life, trying to survive.

He ended up here after hopping a bus from Montreal, stealing along the way to get his next ticket, and this was his last stop. Somehow he had gotten involved with this inner city church, and now he was volunteering to help out with youth who were perhaps where he had once been. Admittedly, I was impressed! I couldn't believe some of the stories he told me about the way his family, especially his mom, had treated him. He told me that there was even a time when he was involved in gangs, and he'd sat outside her home in a vehicle with a gun scoped to her head, aiming to kill her. Then he chickened out and they sped away before anyone knew what they were conjuring up in their plans.

He told me that when he moved here, he met a guy who helped him and started bringing him to this church. It was then that he decided that he didn't want anyone else to grow up the way he did, and that's why he was drawn to the youth in the inner city. I fell in a really "big" way for this guy who had so much compassion for people, especially youth who struggled with the same things he had—youth who really didn't feel like they had any hope.

We met in late 1993. J moved home with me in the late spring of 1994, and that summer we were married. I received my acceptance into the Social Work program that I had been waiting for, so we moved back to central Alberta so I could go to school.

J took to him like a duck to water! We were incredibly happy, doing lots of family things together, the three of us. We spent much of our time outdoors, playing at the kids' park, rollerblading, ice skating, and having adventures through the walking paths in the wilderness parks.

I couldn't actually imagine my life any happier. I was working hard at school. He was working hard at his job. We were going to church together and getting back to our church in Southern Alberta as much as possible. We shared everything in our lives, and our relationship was strong because we could be honest with each other about anything. It was the first time in my life that I truly felt that I had a best friend with whom I could share all the secrets of my heart and feel safe knowing that he honoured me and respected my feelings.

Of course, things weren't always easy. Like most young families, there were financial stresses. My student loan covered basic expenses, and he was working really hard to make up the difference, but we had a beautiful duplex close to J's daycare and my school, and we had really settled into our new life quite well.

In the spring, once I had finished my first year of school, he suggested that we try to find a little house at the lake to rent. We'd recently been broken into, and he thought it would be a safer neighbourhood. I had to admit, it would be nice to be at the lake for the summer, so we did just that. We spent the summer walking along the beach, playing at the park, rollerblading all over town, and enjoying our yard and garden. We were in the prime of our happy threesome when we excitedly discovered that there would be an addition!

CHAPTER SIX—ETERNALLY BROKEN

One afternoon that summer, J and I both lay down for afternoon naps. During my nap, I had a dream about a little girl named D. I don't remember the dream; I just remember waking up and instinctively knowing that if I had a little girl, this was to be her name.

That same afternoon, after J had woken up from her nap, she and I went to the park to play. I was sitting beside a father who was also watching his kids play. We didn't speak really, maybe a "hello," but when he was ready to go, he called out to his daughter, "Okay, D, it's time to go!" Not quite believing my own ears, I turned to him and questioned him about his daughter's name. "Oh," he said, "her name is Danika."

Confused, I quizzed him further, "But that's not what you called her," I said to him.

He said, "Oh, sometimes I call her D for short."

I was flabbergasted. Trying to pick my jaw up from the ground, I explained to him that I'd just had a dream about a little girl with that same name that very afternoon. At that moment, I knew without a doubt that would be the name of my unborn child.

As September approached and the time for school crept up, my husband suggested that it was better to be back in the city rather than so far out for work and school. So we packed up and found a nice home to rent that would be close to J's school and that had an extra room for the baby. I loved that he always wanted what was best for us.

In the next number of months, crazy things would happen to us. My student loan deposits disappeared out of our bank account; I would go to pay a bill, and our account would be empty; I was getting calls from the bank that there were empty envelopes deposited into our account, and the cash withdrawn.

I didn't understand what was happening. My husband told me that there must have been a mix-up and that he would go to the bank and straighten it out. When it happened again, the lady at the bank called me personally, asking me to come in. She took me into a private office and explained to me that she had video of my husband at the ATM depositing the empty envelopes and withdrawing hundreds of dollars at a time.

This was devastating news to me. Shock, unbelief, disbelief, distrust, questions … so many questions … entered into my mind. I was utterly deflated and discouraged. From that moment forward, things would never be the same. Suddenly, I had all of these confusing thoughts and emotions happening in my being all at once.

Our trust was severely compromised. Our friendship started to fall apart. I started noticing other things that he was lying about but that I couldn't really "prove." We were fighting more and more, and this anger, the anger that I thought was long gone, started to stir in me once again.

Then one day I noticed that his wedding ring was gone. This was the big one that struck my anger chord! Finally, he fessed up that he had a gambling problem, bringing some honesty into our relationship. Things started to make sense to me. He told me that he had pawned off his wedding ring so he could have gambling money. Together we went down to the pawn shop and bought back his ring. I told him that I loved him and I would stand behind him and support him, but that he needed to get himself some help; however, the last straw came that January.

I had been anticipating for weeks the day that my lump sum student loan would be deposited so that I could finish my final semester of school. We had desperately needed that money to pay my tuition and bills that had been piling for months, not to mention to start preparing for the arrival of the baby, who was due the beginning of April. I went to the bank first thing, the morning that I knew my payment was coming, so I could take out the money that I needed for some groceries and my tuition. The account was already emptied.

Here I found myself almost seven months pregnant, trying to finish my last few months of school, trying to be strong for J, but extremely broken inside. I told my husband that I couldn't live this way any longer. I told him that I loved him very much, but that he was going to have to get help and move out on his own while he went through this time. I told him that I would support him in whatever way I could, but I needed him to move out. That was a very difficult decision for me. He and J had grown so close, and I really just wanted things to be back to the way that they were. When I asked him to move out, he flat out refused and told me he wasn't going to move out.

Just months' prior, I had finished up my required practicum hours for my Social Work program at the women's shelter. In light of my present situation, and his refusal to move out, I now found myself on the other side of the intake desk, needing a safe place for my daughter and I to stay.

During this time, I'd come back to my house to get some things for school and found my desktop computer missing. I managed to track him down and forced him to show me where it was. I had important school papers on it and all of my work that I needed to submit in order to graduate! He took me to a store in a back alley that he said was a computer repair store and assured me that he was getting it fixed for me.

My head was so messed up at that point that I didn't know what to believe. I wanted to believe the best of my husband. I loved him so much … at least the guy I thought I knew. But there were so many lies and confusing things. As it turned out, I got my computer back and had the locks changed on my house so that he couldn't get in. That forced him to find another place to live, and I came home with J. Out of concern for me, my husband suggested that I wouldn't be able to afford the house on my own, so I should try to find something else. I found a smaller house, big enough for myself, J, and the baby.

The day I moved, he was supposed to come help me with the big stuff so that I didn't have to lift anything while pregnant, but he was a no-show. I called a moving company and explained my situation, and they came that afternoon.

So there I was, almost full-term by now, packing, moving, writing final papers and final exams, and no husband in sight. I had no idea where he'd moved to, and my head was so messed up that I almost didn't know which way was up!

My new landlord was most gracious and agreed to wait for his damage deposit until I had gotten my other one back from my previous landlord. I waited for weeks for a cheque to come in the mail. I finally had contact with my husband and talked to him about it. He assured me that our previous landlord just kept delaying but that he would personally bring it to me as soon as he got it.

Finally, I decided to take matters into my own hands. I found out where our previous landlord's downtown office was, marched into his office, and demanded to see him. I'm thankful that he had some discernment, because with a very confused look on his face, he invited me to speak privately with him in his office. I began relating my plight, stating that I'd waited long enough to get my damage deposit back and couldn't wait any longer, because my new landlord had already been very patient with me.

There he sat unabatingly, waiting for me to finish before he said, "I think there is a misunderstanding, and I need to explain a few things to you." He went on to explain the reality of the situation—that I would not be getting my damage deposit back. He explained that since we'd moved in last fall, we hadn't paid the rent since the first month, and that my husband had kept making excuses about why it was late. He told me that we had been evicted from that home in February.

This was now the end of March. I sat there listening to him in complete and utter disbelief. I felt like I had just been pile-driven by a big Mack truck and was now trying to make sense of my own reality; I was completely blown away.

He discerned the look and the devastation on my face, and I am so thankful that he was very gentle and calm. In his compassion, he explained that he could tell that this was all news to me; therefore, he wouldn't come after me for the months of rent I owed him, but I would certainly not be getting my damage deposit back. I left his office so completely broken. I was humiliated, defeated, deeply disturbed, in shock, and overwhelmed.

As I drove home that day, I didn't know how much more I could take. I had so much on my plate, I felt like I was just a walking zombie. The college was more than gracious with me, helping me out with my finances, classes, papers, exams, and anything else that would help me get through.

My mind kept wandering back to that meeting; it was like an awakening for me. I had no idea that when I gave my husband the money to go pay the rent, it never actually got paid. I started thinking about the months and years previous, all the problems we had, all the times we had moved.

Out of curiosity, I started making phone calls. I called each of our previous landlords and explained who I was and why I was calling. Much to my disbelief, I discovered that each time we'd moved, it really wasn't because he wanted something better for us. It was actually because the rent hadn't been paid for months, and we had been evicted!

In two years, we were broken into four or five times. Putting all the pieces together in my mind, I realized that each time we'd been broken into was a setup so that he could take things of value and pawn them off. It was all making sense! All of these things that had so much meaning for me, like needlework pictures that my grandmother had done for me and J's first pair of cowboy boots, so many precious things of mine, had all been "stolen" in break-ins and discarded to earn him a few dollars. The grief began to set in for me, and my only recourse was to numb myself and get through my final few weeks of school.

Then the thought came to me that I should meet with his employer. After all, I was the one who got him the job through a friend of mine. His employer, a guy I knew through my Social Work program, was surprised to see me. I explained my situation to him and why I was there. He informed me that my husband had been fired six months previous! Dumbfounded at this news, I had all sorts of new questions. Where did he spend all of his nights when he would go out for his night shift for the past six months? After pondering these questions for days and weeks, I decided that I wasn't sure I wanted answers.

I managed to make it through most of my exams, though I ended up dropping a class or two so that I could maintain the GPA that I needed to get into university. My program director and I agreed that I could easily make up the classes in summer session, so this was my plan. Surprisingly, in and amongst all the trials and stress, I still managed to receive the Social Work high achievement award from my class.

Despite the little victories, there was one thing that lingered in me, and I could feel it rising. Though it was a difficult time for me, and I was trying my best to keep it together, I could feel this anger in me that I had once thought was gone for good. It wasn't. Like a black cloud that lingered overhead, it seemed to get darker and darker at the very core of my being. My patience wore thin and my coping skills were lacking. I was not only stressed out to the max, but I was exhausted and deeply wounded. I was deeply grieving the loss of my husband and what I thought was our happy life together. I lost interest in "playing" with J; I was literally hanging on by a thread—angry, confused, hurting.

***

J fell in love with her the moment she laid eyes on her.

"It's a girl! Oh Mommy, she's so precious!"

D. K. arrived in God's perfect time. She was the breath of fresh air that both J and I needed at that time. My beautiful baby girl was just what I needed to give me the strength to go on for the sake of both of my beautiful girls. Although bringing her into our mess certainly wouldn't have been my first choice, she was the sunshine that made our life warm again. J was such a proud big sister and did whatever she could to help me out. My two precious angels that God would use to, once again, console my broken spirit.

Within a week of D's birth, however, it was apparent that there was something wrong. She would stop breathing and begin to almost choke while she was sleeping, and the doctors needed to find out why. Though we were separated, I needed my husband to stay with J at my house so someone was there to care for her and take her to school while I was in the hospital with D. He agreed to do that, and I hoped that maybe it would be a good time of healing for the two of them.

In the mornings, my husband would take J to school and then come up to the hospital to see D and I. I thought and hoped that maybe now having the baby would be enough incentive for him to make the changes that he needed to make so we could be a happy family again. I believed he could do it. After all, he did survive the streets of Montreal and turn his life around, and I was sure he could and would do it again, for us.

One morning while I was still in the hospital with D, my husband came to see me. He wore a grave look on his face. With all sorts of scenarios going on in my head, I asked him what was wrong. He took me to the window in the pediatric ward of the hospital where I was staying with D and pointed across the city to a column of smoke that was barely visible. "I don't know how to tell you this," he said, "but your house burned down this morning."

CHAPTER SIX—ETERNALLY BROKEN

I'm not sure I can actually describe the pain, shock, and numbness that went through my body like a bolt of lightening, all in a matter of seconds. "J?" I asked with terror in my voice. He assured me that she was safe at school. The next thing I knew, this enormous scream of terror erupted from the very core of me. I dropped to my knees and cried out, "No, no, no!" The nurses came rushing into the room to see what the horror was, probably fearing the worst. I couldn't even speak to them. I didn't want to be touched. I didn't want to be consoled. I actually felt like I was losing my mind, like it really wasn't me in this body because, somehow, my mind was so far on overload that I couldn't process.

I couldn't stop the painful cries that came right from the very depth of my being. The nurses tried to calm me, but I didn't want to be touched. I didn't want anyone near me, yet we were in a pediatric ward and they really needed me to be calm. I tried to run from them, to get away. It was absolute chaos. I overheard one of the nurses on the phone trying to get a doctor's order for a shot of valium; two other nurses were pleading with me, chasing me to try to calm me. I was disturbing the entire ward; I was completely out of control of my mind and emotions. I had finally hit my breaking point, and no one could reach me.

After calming me enough to get close to me, one of the nurses managed to give me a shot to calm me down. I needed to talk to my dad; he would know what to say. I called from the pay phone in the ward, even though I was still crying hysterically. He could hardly understand me as he listened tolerantly on the other end of the phone, trying to piece together my broken sentences with their cries of agony.

He was at the farm in Saskatchewan doing spring work at the time that I called. Once I finally managed to get everything out and he understood the magnitude of what had happened, he tried to calm me and said he was on his way. He immediately dropped everything at the farm, got in the truck, and drove the six hours to central Alberta. By the time he arrived, I had J with me at the hospital and I was in a perpetual state of shock.

My dad asked if I had been to the house, and I told him I couldn't go. I just emotionally couldn't handle going. My dad and my husband went together to the house to assess the damage. Dad said it was overwhelming to see and that there wasn't a lot that could be salvaged. What didn't burn was ruined either due to smoke or water damage. He said the fire chief told him it was minutes from engulfing the entire house, but regardless there wouldn't be a lot that could be salvaged. The only blessing in it was that it was such a tiny house, and because I had just moved in, I wasn't completely unpacked, so lots of mine and J's childhood keepsakes were still in the garage out back, untouched.

While Dad was there, he had conversations with the fire chief and the city police. They went through the house together, trying to figure out what had happened. Their conclusion was that the fire had been started by smoking materials. Apparently, the ashtray had been knocked off its holder and had fallen, unnoticed, into a wicker wastepaper basket. We were just thankful that my husband had decided to take the dog with him that morning when he went to drop J off at school.

The next day, my husband was supposed to meet Dad at the house to sort through everything and put whatever they could salvage into the garage until I could deal with things. My husband didn't end up showing up, so my dad spent the day sorting through soot and burnt items, trying to salvage as much as he possibly could.

In the meantime, the local news station had already been up to the hospital to interview us, presenting us as a young couple with a six-year-old daughter and a brand new baby who had lost everything in a house fire with no insurance to cover losses. I was such an emotional wreck, and the fact that my husband and I were separated at the time became irrelevant to me. I desperately needed to lean on him.

After our story hit the six o'clock news, the response was incredibly overwhelming! The donations that came in were astounding: clothes, furniture, baby items, little girl clothes, toys, money, and more money! The nurses on the pediatric ward collected money from the staff at the hospital, and the local fire department took our family shopping. I was touched, overwhelmed, and overburdened all at the same time. I couldn't believe the generosity of people.

Once D was discharged from the hospital, various people put us up in a hotel until we could find a new place. While we were in the hotel, people who represented an Alberta-wide Christian youth conference, known as YC, showed up at our door one evening. Unbeknownst to us, this man and his wife had heard about our situation and took up a free will offering for our family at the Youth Conference. When they brought us this humungous cash gift, I was incredibly overwhelmed. I was moved to tears that someone would do such a thoughtful thing for us; I couldn't even express what I was feeling.

> I felt a wave of emotion come over me, but for the first time in a very long time, it was a comforting emotion, like God had sent these people to show me that He hadn't forgotten about me. He was showing me that there is still good in the world, and that in all of this, I could know that He was still there.

I felt a wave of emotion come over me, but for the first time in a very long time, it was a comforting emotion, like God had sent these people to show me that He hadn't forgotten about me. He was showing me that there is still good in the world, and that in all of this, I could know that He was still there. That experience, and the incredible generosity of so many others, is what pulled me through that time. It was the hope that I so desperately needed for my battered and bruised spirit.

Over the next number of weeks, we literally had thousands of dollars come to us in donations, giving us a chance to get a good start. I had kept very close track of the cash donations, because I knew that I needed to keep temptation from my husband and to be honest, I really didn't trust him. Together we went to the bank with all of the money and met with the bank manager herself. After explaining his gambling history, we all agreed that the money had to go into an account where both of us had to sign to get money out. That way it wouldn't be a temptation to him, and we could then get well established.

A friend of mine found my husband a new job in a nearby town, so we started looking for a place to live in that area. Friends of ours agreed to let us stay with them for a few weeks until we could find and secure a place of our own. Baby step by baby step, we were rebuilding, and I was beginning to feel somewhat safe and secure again in my marriage and in life.

About three days after we settled into our friends' house, while my husband was at work, I found a place for us to rent. Other people were also looking at the house, so I needed to have the damage deposit paid by the end of that workday in order to secure the house. I called the bank to see how I could make that happen, considering that my husband was at work and we both needed to sign on the account. The clerk on the phone sounded confused, so she put me on hold as she tried to sort through things with the manager.

A short time later, the manager that we had previously met with came on the phone. There was an unsteady tone to her voice. "I am sorry, Bonnie," she hesitantly said. "I am not sure what happened here, but this account has been emptied, and it's your husband's signature on the withdrawal slip."

Why I was shocked, I can't really say, but I was. It was another blow to the stomach, and I'd had enough. He had managed to sweet talk the bank clerk and emptied the account. In that moment, I let the phone drop, collapsed to my knees, and wept out of pure exhaustion. I couldn't take anymore; I knew I had to get out. I told my friends that I had to leave; I had to go back to Saskatchewan to get my head straightened out.

I felt terrible for putting them in this position. No one knew when, or if, he would come back, and I hated that I had endangered their family, but the fear in me was telling me that I needed to go. I called my friend who had gotten him his job to let her know I was leaving and I was sorry, but I didn't know what would happen with his job. She said it was okay and that she had already known that he hadn't shown up for a single day of work yet.

"Really?" I responded, confused. *So where did he actually spend his days that week?* I thought to myself. Honestly, I didn't care anymore.

I packed up the few things that I had, and my friends helped me load up J and the baby. I left Alberta that day with my two girls and nothing to my name. I wept from the deepest part in my soul all the way home to Saskatchewan. How could I have been so stupid to trust him again? I would arrive home, to my parents, broken and confused. I actually just felt numb; I couldn't allow myself to feel anything, or I knew I would break.

I knew he would try to contact me, and he did. His lies continued—lies about the money, lies about everything. When his attempts failed, he would have friends, pastors, priests, even nuns, phone me to try and reach me. They would start out the conversation with concern for me, and then would start to plead his case for him. It was making me even more crazy, and it got so bad that I couldn't handle talking to anyone. My parents screened all my calls, and I literally talked with no one on the phone for months. Like an injured dog too exhausted to even lick my wounds, I just wanted to crawl into a hole and die.

Once I moved home, I was on twenty-four-hour suicide watch. Even though we lived at the lake, my parents had set up a network of counsellors who lived at or near the lake who were willing to be on call if I ever needed someone in a crisis. We had worked out a system that if I was feeling suicidal, I just had to say one word and my mom was on the phone. Within minutes, a counsellor would be at my side. This system saved my life more than once over the next few months, and I was so grateful to these women who were willing to give up their summer holiday time for me, sometimes at the drop of a hat.

My lawyer was fighting the custody side of things for me. He didn't waste any time getting a restraining order and an order for full custody with no access for my husband to either of my girls. There was even a point when my husband tried to gain full custody of my two girls with no access for me to my children. As absurd as that sounds, he had his lawyer in Alberta completely convinced that I was a psychopath who had stolen his children.

My lawyer was exasperated trying to convince his lawyer that he was a con artist and was simply yanking his chain. It wasn't until my husband was a no-show in court and his bill went unpaid that his lawyer actually phoned my lawyer to apologize for putting me through any more stress than I'd already endured in the months previous. My lawyer fought for me like I was one of his own children, and I was so thankful for him. He also absorbed all of my costs, which next to protecting my children was invaluable to me.

At home, we settled into a routine where my mom would get up with D in the night and bring her to me to nurse and then pick her up and put her back in the crib when she was done nursing. I was so depressed that I literally was emotionally numb, and day and night I just lay there when the baby cried, like I was in a whole other world of my own, unaware of the needs of anyone around me. I was emotionally numb to both of my kids for many months to follow. My parents cared for my children, and for me as well, like I was a little girl who had slipped back into the confinement of childhood.

The nightmare would not end there, however. Within a few weeks after I'd moved home, the city police from Alberta phoned both my dad and I separately. They talked about things that dad reported had burned in the fire, and they said that some of those things were showing up in pawn shops in the city. The officer wanted us to come back so we could identify the items and so they could interview us more extensively. I got off the phone baffled at the conversation, trying to process it all. As I sat on the front deck looking out over the lake, it hit me like a ton of bricks! "HE STARTED THE FIRE!" I announced out loud. I called my dad at the farm, "Dad, do you think he could have started it?"

"I was just thinking the same thing as I was putting things together in my mind," he replied.

The two of us and D left that day for Alberta. Sure enough, lots of my things that Dad had reported to the fire department had burned were in pawn shops, including the baby's crib. After extensive meetings with the city police, who at this point really wanted to nail him for arson, it was concluded that because the initial fire reports stated that the fire was started by "smoking material with no accelerants," they couldn't go after him.

He knew exactly what he was doing. Presumably, he took J to school that day, came back to my house, loaded everything from my house that he could get money for, took the dog with him, and left the house. Somehow in all the commotion before he left the house, the ashtray was "accidentally" knocked off its holder into the wicker basket of papers, and it went without notice. I suppose it could have been the dog.

Sometime in all the happenings of his busy morning, my husband found time to go to the pawn shop, sell all of my stuff, and come back to my house, miraculously in just enough time to realize that the house was on fire, heroically calling the fire department to report the emergency!

I may as well have been a boxer, because I was getting to the point in my life that blows to the stomach like this just made me stand taller and fight harder. After we were done at the police station, we decided to go back to the house and load up what was left in the garage, take it home, and be done with Alberta.

I had called some friends to arrange for them to help us lift some of the heavier things. When we arrived, it was the first time that I had seen the half-burnt house. I had prepared myself emotionally to see the house, but I wasn't prepared for what was to come next. As we swung open the double wooden doors of the old shed out back, where everything that I had left in the world was stored, we discovered that it was empty.

It wasn't hard to find him. He was lying on the couch at his buddy's house watching TV when we pulled up in front of the neighbour's house. Through the front window we could see that he was very jumpy and paranoid, peering out the window at every little sound and movement. As he settled back into his lounging position on the couch, we sat in the truck with our eye on his every move as we planned our strategy. One of my friends would stay in the truck with me and the baby; my dad would go to the front door, and my other friend would go to the back in case he tried to run out that way. I sat in the truck, scared, but watching intently.

I don't often see my dad mad, but when my husband answered that front door and slowly cracked it open to peek out, unsure if he should open it all the way, my dad didn't give him any chance to react. In a matter of half a second, my dad had him by the throat with his leviathan arms bulging at every muscle as he hung my husband up against the wall with his feet dangling inches from the floor.

It actually shocked me how strong my dad was, and I could tell he was fighting to restrain himself. He gave my husband a few shakes and a few stern warnings before he released him and let his feet touch the ground again. My dad managed to calm down, and he spent the next few hours trying to reason with my husband and get the answers out of him as to where he'd taken all my stuff. He said he didn't know where it was … just that he sold it. Reasoning with him was futile, so before we left that night, my dad told him that he would come and pick him up the next day and together they would go find it, because we weren't leaving this city without it.

Not surprisingly, that evening my husband was up to his old tricks, trying to manipulate me by checking himself into the psych ward at the hospital on suicide watch. He told the staff that he would not harm himself if he could see me. I refused to go; instead, my dad went. My dad finally got it out of him where the contents of the garage were; apparently, he had sold all of my stuff to an auction company. We spent the next few days driving around to all the auction places in the city and finally found my things. Everything I had left in the world—my childhood memories and J's childhood memories—were still loaded on the five ton truck.

They were just starting to unload the truck when we arrived. My dad explained the situation to the guys that owned the company and told them that he would buy everything back for the price that they bought it for, and he would pay them to drive the truck to Saskatchewan and drop it all off at our farm. But that wasn't going to stop them from unloading all my stuff and selling it in their auction later that day.

My dad pleaded with them, but they said it wasn't their problem. My dad patiently thanked him, walked back to his truck, and dialled the city police. He talked to the officer who was familiar with my case and explained the situation. The officer didn't need much convincing at all!

The police officer didn't interfere; in fact, he didn't even get out of his vehicle. He simply parked his police car across the road in clear view to the owner of the auction company. My dad approached the owner again with his proposal and was successful in convincing the auction owner to sell the entire truckload of stuff to him and have his driver drive it back to Saskatchewan for us.

Over the next weeks and months, I became extremely fearful. The phone calls from my husband, or people he'd convinced to phone on his behalf, were relentless. People couldn't understand how I could be so cold towards this man who was so broken and suicidal, how I could take away his kids, and why I wouldn't even give him the chance to talk with me.

In the back of my mind was the memory of the awful stories he had told me about how he wanted to take revenge on his mom, and how he sat outside of her window with a scope to her head, with the intent to kill her because of the way she'd treated him as a child. I began to imagine what he might do to me or my children. It would be six months before I would finally force myself to go to the store for milk. I remember the first time that I went to the local grocery store. Like a rabbit being hunted by a fox, I crept around the aisles, convinced that he was hiding in the next aisle and had been waiting for me to leave the safety of my parents' home.

When I was home, I was even afraid to let the girls play on the beach out front, because I feared that he was lingering around, just waiting for his opportune moment to try and take them. Slowly over the next number of months, I progressed to going to town on my own, being able to drive myself to my counselling sessions, and then even taking my kids out for walks and around town.

In the months after I left Alberta, as I became more relaxed and settled, I started thinking about all of the people who possibly may have been negatively affected by my life over the past few years, unbeknownst to me, but due to his lies and manipulations. I made a list and started making phone calls. I just wanted to be honest and up front and make amends with people who had been negatively affected and possibly had hard feelings. I needed to have a fresh start and make everything right that I possibly could. I also didn't want people to find out things from other people; I would rather have it came from me.

I contacted as many people as I could think of: previous landlords, friends, people who had helped us out. Most were very empathetic, though some reacted like they had been instant victims of my circumstances. I couldn't be responsible for that, but I had to have a clean slate and start over, even if that meant some people were angry with me.

I contacted my ex-husband's mom in Montreal. Yes, the mother he told me was dead. In the first year of our marriage, on Christmas Day, he was talking in French to someone on the phone. When he got off, I asked him who he was talking to, and he nonchalantly told me that it was his mom. I was quite offended that he had kept this hidden from me, and that he was acting like it was nothing for me to make a big deal out of.

He explained himself by saying that he had hated her so much, that in his mind he considered her dead but now that he was married and was settled, he was thinking of her. He was ready to forgive and wanted to call. I accepted his explanation and didn't question it again, because I was actually proud that he was able to face her in love and forgiveness. In my mind, it was the beginning of rebuilding a relationship that had been broken far too long.

Anyhow, now that I had left him, and the girls were safe, I wanted her to hear from me what had happened. I wanted her to know that I would love to stay in contact with her for the girls' sake. Much to my surprise, his mom was relieved to receive my phone call. She was happy to hear that I had gotten out of my marriage with him. She told me that she and her family had been afraid for me and my children, but didn't know how to communicate with me. Their English was very poor, and they didn't know how to tell me the truth about him, because they didn't know how I would take it.

Throughout our very long and interesting conversation of broken English, the first truth that I learned was that he didn't actually grow up on the streets of Montreal. She told me that he was raised in a very good home; he wasn't raised by his grandmother because his mother had beat him, like he had told me. He was, in fact, raised with both parents, but he was always causing trouble in the home by lying, manipulating, and stealing. She told me that she had been very concerned for me and my girls because of her son's past behaviour, but she had hoped that he had changed. There were a whole lot of things that I found out in that conversation, things I wish I never knew. Interestingly enough, she also told me that he made a habit of meeting vulnerable women at churches, sweet talking them, and then using them for money, vehicles, or anything he could get his hands on. She apologized profusely for not telling me sooner, but she was happy to hear that my girls and I were safe. I thanked her for her concern, and I assured her that she'd done the right thing, because I probably wouldn't have believed her prior to this point in time anyway.

CHAPTER SIX—ETERNALLY BROKEN

After I got off the phone with her, I was once again a numb wreck. The immensity of the situation took a long time to sink in. My whole being was in shock as I realized that, in addition to all I had just been through, everything he'd ever told me was a lie.

This man whom I had loved so deeply—the man I chose to give all of my heart to and not hold anything back, was not the man that I knew. He had been an imposter in my heart, in my home, and in my family. I felt like my heart would be eternally broken. My wounds were so deep, I knew I would never be the same again.

Chapter Seven

STOP THIS RIDE, I WANT OFF!

For many months to come, I found myself on a path of healing, a path of trying to find my purpose and my direction. I was trying to find where I could fit into this world and do something right. I was so broken inside, I don't even remember a lot of the initial six months after I left Alberta. I remember certain things because I have some pictures. I remember nursing D in a rocking chair with a blank stare. I remember feeling chronically numb, like I was dead inside but somehow functioning in this body. My life for almost a whole year was comprised of counselling sessions, self-help meetings, coffee dates with other women who had been victims, and caring for my kids. Anything else would have been too much for me to handle.

As crisis and despair became less prevalent in my life, I began the long, hard journey of trying to rebuild, picking up the shattered pieces of my life. My mind often fought suicidal thoughts, thoughts of how my kids deserved a better mom, how I'd never shake this victim feeling, and how I'd never find someone who would want me with all my broken pieces. I often felt like I had a big stamp on my forehead that said "Victim. Please dump here!"

At the same time, I was making great strides working through things with my counsellor and in my self-esteem classes. I was starting to put all the broken pieces back together, but there was this thing … this void. It was still there.

About a year after I moved home, I was ready to become independent again. I started working, found low-income housing, and lived on my own with my kids. Fear still gripped my life, especially when the kids were playing outside or when J was walking to school by herself, but I chose to move forward in confidence. To be honest, though it became less intense, the fear of my ex-husband lurking around the next corner never left me until twenty years later, on D's wedding day, when I knew she was in the care and safety of her loving husband, and I could finally let go.

***

Almost two years after my life was shattered from my first marriage, I met up with a guy I had known from high school at a Christmas party. He was quite a bit older than I, and we weren't ever close friends, but we knew each other. He seemed interested in charming me, and I wasn't sure how I felt about that.

I talked it over with my counsellor and my support group, and everyone thought it was too early for me to get involved with someone, yet I had a hard time resisting his charm, and he insisted that I shouldn't ignore his advances or his phone calls. I chose to go against the advice of the people who saw that my healing was not complete, and I caved in to my need to belong, to be loved.

Our courting time was short, our engagement was short, and so was our marriage. I knew in my heart that it wasn't right, but by the time the wedding day came around, I didn't have the confidence or the strength of character to call it off.

Reflecting back now, I realize that I could see all the warning signs, but I wanted to believe all the charming things he said. I really just wanted someone to love me. I think I could see the truth of our relationship and how it would end, but I was confused by his charm and my deep needs and desires.

The night before the wedding, a close friend of mine stayed at our place and heard us fighting all night. In the morning she asked if I was

CHAPTER SEVEN—STOP THIS RIDE, I WANT OFF!

sure that I wanted to do this. I told her that everything was fine, even though in my heart I knew it wasn't. I literally cried all the way down the aisle on our wedding day, because deep in my heart I knew I was making a huge mistake.

For our honeymoon we went camping, and we took my two little girls with us. J was eight years old by then, and D was two. We decided to just get in the vehicle and drive … it would be a trip of adventure!

We couldn't agree on where to camp, and I had valid reasons for not wanting to go west of Calgary: I had spent a family vacation there with my ex-husband, and I didn't want to go back. Yet that is where my new husband wanted to go. We were still fighting when we left Calgary.

He got so angry with me that he drove the truck off the road, hit a highway marker and the edge of an approach, and then slammed on the brakes and skidded to a stop on the top of the approach. I got out of the truck, took my two scared little girls out of the back seat, grabbed my purse, and slammed the door.

He spit gravel as he sped away, burning rubber on the pavement for a long way down the highway as he drove away in a rage. I walked down the highway with my two little girls, one on my hip, one by the hand, all three of us crying, and me wondering how I'd ended up in this position.

As we made our way up a gravel road to get away from the traffic of the busy highway, a truck driven by an older Indigenous man stopped. He could tell that we had all been crying, and he was very kind. He said to me, "Ma'am, you do not want to go any further on this road with those two little girls. Over that hill is a very tough reservation, and trust me, you do not want to go there."

I thanked him and had no other choice but to turn around and head back towards the busy highway. I could see my husband parked on the side of the road a fair distance away, waiting to see what I would do. The only choice that I could see at that point was to get back in with him and try to work it out.

After that trip, I would come to realize very quickly that I should've listened to my gut and to my counsellor's advice. I would put my children through scarring situations that no child should ever have to witness. I was too naïve, too needy, and too vulnerable to have the courage to stop it. His fits of rage and jealously would become the norm in our home, seemingly triggered by whatever mood he was in. It was wrong on so many levels, and the ones it hurt the most were my children.

For some reason, I had the mindset that I didn't deserve any better. I felt that I desperately needed him in my life, because maybe no one else would want me. He had me convinced that he was my knight in shining armour that would save me, even though he was the one who was draining me. He was draining my home of the joy that we had found once again, draining my bank account, draining my time with my children, and draining my emotions with his fits of rage.

One night at my staff party, he went into a jealous fit and dragged me out to our vehicle so he could "discuss" things with me. While we were in the parking lot, he threw me into the side of the vehicle a number of times, yelling at me because I was having too much fun and leaving him out. A guy I worked with had followed us outside because he'd seen my husband drag me out. Shortly after my husband started throwing me around, this guy made his presence known by clearing his throat so my husband knew that he was there. He pretended to busy himself with something, but I know that is what stopped my husband from getting too out of control.

After that night, it would take two major fights, being physically thrown around my home in front of my children, being pushed into doors and walls, and seeing the fear in the eyes of my two little girls before I finally told him to move out.

At one point during the second fight, I was trying to get past him and out of my bedroom before things escalated. As I tried to walk past him, he lay on the bed with his feet closest to my side of the bed. As I walked past, he kicked me so hard in the hips that it dropped me to my knees instantly in pain. He knew that my hips were my "weakest link," considering I had pelvic injuries from a car accident in high school. Pain shot through my legs, but I managed to get up off the floor and run to the living room to grab the phone. My kids were in hysterics by this time, and I knew my only option was to call the police to intervene and stop him from continuing in his rage.

CHAPTER SEVEN—STOP THIS RIDE, I WANT OFF!

When the police arrived, they immediately sent him away and then questioned me as to the events of the evening. They asked if I wanted to press charges, so I went through with the procedure of doing that. His father, a retired RCMP officer, obviously knew the ins and outs of legal loopholes, so he advised his son on how to handle the situation, and they answered those charges with a threat to press charges of their own unless I dropped mine.

It was my word against his. I went to the police station, dropped my charges, then went directly to my lawyer's office to have the marriage annulled. Within six months of our wedding, it was over. I had finally found the courage, and I decided I was not going to live the rest of my life in fear, nor was I going to let my children suffer in this situation anymore.

My life was a mess again. I believe that by this time in my life, a lot of people had given up on me. The destructive choices that I continued to make were extremely damaging to me and to my girls. How much more could my kids take? How much more could I take? Everyone wanted to see me and my girls happy, but here I was again in a situation that was so unhealthy. Neediness. Emptiness. Abuse. Divorce. Anger. Shame. Depression. Suicidal. Neediness. Emptiness. Abuse. Divorce. Anger. The cycle continued. I just wanted this ride to stop! Just stop this ride and let me off!

Chapter Eight

COWBOY ... TAKE ME AWAY

When you live your life as a victim, whether it be a victim of your circumstances, the past, or your own emptiness, you unwittingly seek to fill the neediness you have in the depth of your core. In doing that, you inadvertently attract people who haven't found acceptance elsewhere for whatever reason of their own. Unfortunately, those people are usually just as, if not more, unhealthy as you are, even if both of you look "all together" on the outside.

This time, I chose well! He came from a Christian home, and I'd known him previously. His sister and I were best friends in university; in fact, she was J's godmother. The security of choosing a man like this had pretty good odds. He was the one who had witnessed the way my husband was treating me that night in the parking lot at our staff party. Since then, he seemed to have his eye out for me and my best interest in mind. I actually felt safer going and coming from work knowing that there was someone who knew what I was going through and would keep an eye out for me.

What I didn't know until later was that he was actually waiting for the papers of my divorce to go through before he would ask me out. Once we started dating, it seemed like I had finally arrived. I had finally started to make some right choices! We dated for quite some time, and my girls became very attached to him. They really needed a daddy who would love them, and I needed a man who would love me and take care of me the way I deserved to be taken care of.

The second spring that we were dating, we eloped. He was a cowboy and a pasture manager, so once we were married, the girls and I moved to the pasture where he worked, and we excitedly began our happy little life together. He was my cowboy … and he took me away.

I loved country life; it's in my blood. It warmed my heart watching my kids playing at the barn, or for endless hours in the dirt and in the trees, where their biggest concern was keeping their kitties safe from the luring owls. I loved watching through the kitchen window as my husband, his rider, and our girls, would all ride out for the afternoon together to check cows.

Rodeo became a way of life for us on the weekends and there weren't many weekends at home from May to October. If we weren't working on the ranch or in the garden, we were "playing" on the rodeo grounds. Roping nights became common around our place, and there was always beer in the fridge.

Spring, summer, and fall kept the girls and I busy for hours working in our one acre garden—planting, weeding, harvesting, canning, freezing, pickling, preserving. In the winter, my favourite thing to do was cook, but I also loved to sew, do crafts with the kids, and cross-stitch.

For the first time in my life I was a stay at home mom, and I loved it! We were a perfect little family. We even went to church on Sundays! I really was living my dream. Finally, I had managed to break this cycle. Finally, I'd made it.

From the outside looking in, even at times from the inside looking out, we were a happy, perfect little family, and things couldn't be any better in my life. We were the perfect *Country Woman Magazine* family … at least that's how other people described us.

About six months into our marriage, things slowly started taking a turn for the worse. Actually, it really only took one incident that would change things forever. When we were dating, he had once said to me that he wasn't sure if we should get married, because he was really scared of his "dark" side. I couldn't even imagine him having a dark side, so I told him I thought it was ridiculous! But then his "dark side" reared its ugly head one day. We were having an argument … about what, I'm not even sure … and as I walked past him in the dining room, he shoved me into the wall.

That shove was enough to paralyze me completely. Instantaneously, the emotional shock felt like I had just been jolted back into a nightmare in time, like a cat reacting to danger with her back arched and hair standing on end; my instinct was to protect and survive.

I knew from experience that striking back only got me beat up, and quite frankly, I don't think I did or said anything. I was too dumbfounded at this new behaviour from him. The trust that we had built was shaken in that instant. Later that evening, we sat down and I said to him, "We can talk through anything, but please don't physically handle me like that when we fight. I can't handle that. It's like being thrust back into the past, and I can't go there."

As we sat and discussed things, it was essential to me that he fully understood how important this was to me. I needed him to know how vulnerable I was about physical fighting, and I needed him to understand the emotional scabs that I carried from my previous marriages. Unbeknownst to me, that conversation was like giving him the keys to "what makes Bonnie crazy."

Even though we had talked things through that night, over the following days and weeks, lingering fear was my constant companion. Something had shifted in our relationship. My senses were on overload trying to read situations and conversations, and making sure I didn't make a wrong move or say the wrong thing, so as to make him react. My head swirled with confusing thoughts, doubts, and questions.

My heart ached, and the feeling of betrayal was overwhelming; I could once again feel my spirit closing up, capturing itself back into the cocoon from where it had just emerged. It was about this time that the criticism really started. At first, I thought it was just normal for couples to fight like this, but I should've figured it out when I discovered that his parents were having private conversations with him about concerns they had about me. That's also when the fighting started to escalate. It wouldn't be long before I'd become well acquainted with that dark side he once spoke about, but it was too late now. I was committed.

***

"Come on, J ... keep up with mommy." I struggled to talk and walk at the same time. I was exhausted from fighting with my husband, and I was now drudging my way across the stubble field with a four-year-old on one hip and a ten-year-old struggling to keep up.

"Hurry, J," I tried patiently to encourage her. I wasn't sure where I was going to take the girls ... perhaps the neighbours' house a mile away. J was exhausted from crying during the fight, and was more scared than anything.

"Mommy, does this mean we're leaving Daddy?" D asked in her scared little four- year-old voice.

"I don't know, sweetie ... I don't know ... let's just get to the neighbours and figure things out from there." I tried to reassure her without letting her know just how scared I was.

"But Mommy, I don't want to leave Daddy," she pleaded with me.

"I know, sweetie ... I know." I blankly answered her as the question of how I ended up in this situation again crossed my mind.

"Come on now, J, just keep walking." I could see the lights of the truck coming down the road. The moonlight was bright enough to give us away in the field, but I had to keep going, hoping that he would just keep driving down the road and not see us in the field to the north of the gravel road. The truck crept past us and kept going slowly down the road as I had the girls lay down in the stubble and keep still.

Whew, I thought. But I knew he'd be back when he didn't find us down the road.

"Mommy, why was Daddy being so mean to you?" D asked.

As flashes of what happened earlier went through my head, I tried to remember where it all started. What had made him so mad to start with? Oh yeah, I spent too much money on groceries again. Lost in my thoughts, I wandered back in my mind ...

"I told you that you have an allowance of $300.00 a month for groceries. Why do you keep buying all these extra things? We don't need all these extra things, like ava-f—ing-cado! I've never even heard of ava-f—ing-cado! If you can't spend only the money that I allow you for groceries, then I'll go buy the f—ing groceries, and you can cook with what I give you. Do you f—ing understand me?"

"Yes," I argued, "but I can't cook the things that you like unless I get the ingredients that I need."

"Well, you'll just have to f—ing make do! My mother made do, just fine, and so can you!" He yelled back even louder to make sure he got his point across.

The next thing I knew, I felt myself hit hard against the wall. That was all I could take. I wasn't scared anymore. I screamed back in his face, challenging him. "Don't ever lay your hands on me! Don't ever lay your hands on me again!"

I knew that I was really no threat at all. I knew it would just make him crazier, but I couldn't take any more, and I wasn't going to let my kids stand there watching me be tossed around again and not fight back.

He pounced towards me. This time he was towering over me, shoving me backwards by both shoulders. "Why, what are you going to do? Go running home to Mommy and Daddy?" He shoved me again. This time harder than ever; I stumbled backwards towards the fridge.

By this time my two little girls were crying hysterically, trying to get close to protect me, but keeping a safe distance as they followed him and watched him taunt me with little shoves backwards while he screamed in my face.

"Daddy, what are you doing? Leave Mommy alone," J said with real ten-year-old authority, yet terror, in her voice. My two little girls huddled together and then shuffled their way around us into the front porch as he backed me up as far as he could into the fridge. They had never seen their new step-daddy this mad before, and they were terrified.

"What do you mean don't touch you? I'll shove you if I f—ing feel like shoving you!" He gave me a final shove into the fridge. He was getting himself really worked up now. I had never seen him this angry, and he was really getting out of control.

"Okay … I get it. Can you just stop now?" I tried to calm him, but he just got more and more worked up.

His voice was almost at a scream, and he wasn't stopping now. "In fact, this is MY f—ing house, MY f—ing kitchen, and MY f—ing yard.

If I want to shove you, I'll f—ing shove you!" He shoved me back again, this time throwing me into the hallway of the front entrance.

J shouted again, "Stop it!" I knew the girls were scared, but I couldn't concern myself with them right now. I was trying to wrap my brain around how to calm him down.

He shoved me backwards again. I tried to keep my balance amongst all the shoes in the entrance and somewhat stand my ground. "Okay, what are you doing? Enough already!" I shouted.

He was relentless by now and completely unforgiving. He went on, "In fact, I'll shove you right out of MY f—ing house if I want to!"

I fought to keep myself from getting pushed right out the door. He kept backing me up closer and closer to the door with each shove. The girls were hysterical by now, but also completely helpless. Little D was screaming and crying, and J took on the role of consoling her, trying to protect and calm her little sister, who was hysterical with fear.

He was completely out of control by now. He opened the door, and as he towered over me and reached to throw the screen door open, he yelled "Are you happy now? You can just stay out of MY f—ing house!"

He gave me one last shove, right out of the house and backwards into the railing on the tiny front porch. As I caught myself from falling down the stairs, he slammed the door and locked it. I could hear my little girls on the inside of the door screaming with terror for him to open the door and let their mommy in. He was yelling back at them, "If your mom wants to be a b—ch like that, she belongs outside … and she can stay there!"

I stood out on the front porch and looked around the yard to see if the hired man was around. It was almost dusk, but there was still plenty of light to see across the yard. Sure enough, there he was standing at the doors of the barn, looking over to the house to see what all the commotion was about. When our eyes met, he bowed his head under his cowboy hat and walked back into the barn, so as to mind his own business. He wasn't about to go interfering in his bosses' personal stuff … he was just the rider, and he wanted it to stay that way.

I stood on the porch for a few minutes, not knowing what to do. I was crying by this time, and it felt like my heart was being ripped out of my chest. I could hear my kids screaming.

CHAPTER EIGHT—COWBOY...TAKE ME AWAY

"Let my mommy in!" D screamed. "Mommy, Mommy!"

I banged on the door again, almost going crazy with emotion. Should I try the front door? No, the air-conditioner was in the front screen, and the door couldn't be opened. I banged on the door. "C'mon, let me in the house! Can't you see you're scaring the girls! Let me in!"

"Shut up!" he shouted back. "The girls are f—ing fine! You're the problem, not them!"

At that, I broke down. I sat down on the top step and dropped my head between my knees and wept. How could I have possible gotten myself and my girls into this kind of a mess again? What was I going to do? He was probably right ... I was the problem! After all that my kids had been through, how could this possibly be happening again? I sat there for a few minutes and tried to gather my thoughts. *I've got to get out of here*, I thought. *I've got to get my girls and get out of here!* Hearing my little girls on the other side of that door screaming in terror was killing me... ripping my very heart out! I gathered myself together and decided it was time to play a new game.

"Okay, listen. I'm sorry that I spent too much money on the groceries. I just wanted to make you a nice meal, and I got carried away. I'm sorry. Please let me in the house. The girls are scared ... please." I pleaded with him and waited in silence for a few minutes to see if there was a response.

I heard the unlocking of the door and held myself back from shoving the door open before he could change his mind. I waited patiently until he opened the door, but before he let me in, he gestured to the key hanger and made sure I knew that he had taken all the keys off the hooks for the vehicles.

He walked away in a calm, cool, and controlled manner, sending me the message that he would be the one who called the shots around here. We waited until we could hear that he was far enough away before the three of us reunited with a big embrace. My two girls clenched to my body like they would never let me go again.

We could hear his footsteps in the living room and then the TV turn on. Thoughts raced through my head. I still had the sense of panic and felt the need to get out. I felt like my world was crashing in, and I just needed to get away and think. I needed to clear my head and gather my thoughts. I was so confused ... I needed to run.

All the keys were gone. *What will I do? Where will I go?* I whispered to the girls to get their shoes on and I helped little D with hers. We quietly slipped out the door. It was dark enough now that we could get away through the trees without being seen.

As we crouched now, hiding in the stubble field, I watched as he got to the end of the road and waited to see what he was going to do. He knew that not enough time had passed for us to get too far, but I was hoping that he would turn and go further down the road to give us time to get into the low part of the field. No luck ... he got to the end of the road and I watched the truck lights turn around. Panic struck me. *Oh no*, I thought, *he's sure to see our silhouettes.* I knew we were on the high ground of the stubble field.

As the truck got closer, I told the girls to get down low and just stay still. The truck passed, and I thought we may be safe, but the truck turned into the approach of the field and I knew that he had spotted us. He headed up the field straight towards us, and I panicked at a loss of what to do next. J and D realized what was happening and started to cry.

"Mommy, he saw us. What are we going to do?"

He drove slow and steady towards us, letting me know that he knew exactly where we were, but with a calmness that made me think he'd maybe come to his senses. I didn't know what else to do, so I just kept walking with the girls towards the neighbours' house as I scrambled in my mind about what to do next.

As the truck got closer, my panic increased. I was scared of what he would do. I could hear desperation in his voice as he called my name from the passenger side window, which was rolled down. "Bonnie, what are you doing? What are you doing, Bonnie? Come on, Bonnie. Where are you going? Okay, I'm sorry I lost my cool. Bonnie, come on. Come back to the house."

I was relieved that his outburst was over, but I knew that no matter what decision I made at this point, I would never trust him again. I felt betrayal and fear; I didn't know who this man was anymore. This was not the man that I married ... or was it?

CHAPTER EIGHT—COWBOY…TAKE ME AWAY

***

We often had people over to our house, which was a relief for me, because then there was beer and no fighting. No one knew what actually happened in our house, except my children. I became very good at hiding behind the "country woman" image, and my own shame. The way I saw it, I was committed, and he constantly reminded me that I was the one who'd been married twice before, not him, so he was obviously not the problem.

Even though much was hidden in our home, I soon learned that my only chance of survival was to allow the anger that was buried deep inside to come to the surface and fight back. The rage that I had been trying to exterminate deep within, since my childhood, would not remain hidden in the midst of his scathing criticism. That rage rose up in me during those five years we were married, and together we created this volatile, violent, emotionally toxic home where my kids tried to find a meagre peaceful existence, but where broken hopes, dreams, and promises filled their memory books.

Over those five years, our fighting escalated from those first simple shoves into the wall to him throwing me down stairs and me running back up to knee him where it counted. I decided that I'd taken enough from men, and there was no way I was just going to sit back and take it anymore. They say it takes two to fight, and it's true. And fight we did.

Somewhere in the middle of it all, I do believe that we really did love each other, and like most people in an unhealthy marriage, we gave an honest effort at trying to reconcile and make things work. It wasn't all anger; there was laughter and good memories too. We were, however, just two lost, hurting, angry people without hope. I think we both thought that maybe the bond of sharing a child would be what we needed to make it work. Selfish? Probably. But I was in too deep to see that.

> If I've learned ONE THING in life, it's this: God is sovereign over ALL.

We lost one baby by miscarriage, but shortly after that, I found myself pregnant again. After a stressful, unstable pregnancy, God blessed us. If I've learned ONE THING in life, it's this: God is sovereign over ALL. In His perfect time, in the marrow of our messy life, God gifted us with another little angel, a beautiful baby girl named R. J. Here I found myself again so in awe of this gift of life from God, and the plans that I know He surely has for each of my girls.

***

Anger, as I've said, is deeply embedded hurt that doesn't know how to express itself. At the root of it is shame. I was full of shame as a child. I was angry as a teenager. I was angry after my first husband, and I was even more angry after my second husband. But this … this would raise up a rage inside of me, like a tsunami that grows and increases in strength and destruction as it advances mile upon mile. I was once again the victim of my own circumstances, once again the victim of my own pain, once again the victim of my own shame, and once again the victim of my own choices, a mom who compromised her own children's well being to find happiness in another empty and abusive relationship! Only this time, I fought back tooth and nail. I had become a fighter, and I wasn't going to let my kids think it was okay to be treated this way. Yet instead of leaving, I did the only other thing I could do—pretend.

A large part of my heart, perhaps even all of it, wanted this life to work. Perhaps that's why it took me five long and painful years to admit that it was really only false hope and shame that made me stay. I knew he was no longer my cowboy, and I no longer wanted him to take me away.

Chapter Nine

FATHER'S LOVING HAND

Emergency medicine was always a passion of mine, but it was something I never believed I could do. During this time, however, I decided I was going to do what I'd always dreamed of and take my Primary Care Paramedic course.

I'd had just about enough of being on my husband's "allowance." He wanted a housewife, and I wanted to be one, but I was tired of being treated like one of the children. My paramedic training was very intense, and it required me to be away at school every second weekend for a full year in order to do distance learning.

The small Saskatchewan town where my course was facilitated was an oil town, and it was expensive to stay in a motel each weekend. However, this small town also had a beautiful, large convent that was occupied by only three nuns. Through a local connection, we were encouraged to approach the nuns about letting some of us out of town women stay at the convent as opposed to a motel.

The first time approaching the doors of the convent was a little intimidating. We went to the side door, rang the buzzer, and waited with still hearts for someone to answer. Within minutes, a nun approached to the door with some caution, but she seemed relieved to see three young women standing at the door awaiting her arrival.

She let us in, and we stood there in the small foyer, explaining our situation to her and posing our proposal about the three of us staying at the convent for two nights every second weekend for the entire year. The nun seemed fairly intrigued and said she would have to discuss it with her sisters and pray about it before she could give us an answer.

As it turned out, the nuns welcomed us to stay with them, and it became "home" for me every second weekend for the entire year for a meagre $10.00/night. Those weekends, I believe, became a time that not only we, but the nuns, looked forward to. Often they would cook a meal for us, and the six of us would share that time together getting to know each other and sharing stories and laughter.

My time at the convent became precious time to me. It was my time of sanctuary, and it was the only place in the world where I could legitimately go by myself and be free from the constant fighting. There was something eerie about that big, empty dormitory, but there was also something peaceful and serene about it. As the weeks went on and I became more comfortable with my surroundings, I was continually drawn to the small chapel which was near to the room that became known as "Bonnie's room."

I had the privilege of occupying what used to be the priests' quarters, so I had easy access to the chapel and began to spend my evenings, and sometimes the middle of the night, privately in the front of the chapel on my knees. I'm convinced that it was the prayers of those beautiful nuns that drew me to the feet of Jesus Himself. For the first time in my life, I took the time to humble myself before the Lord and "be still." I began to cry out to God; I began to turn and face Him. For the first time in my life, I would begin to see and acknowledge my mistakes and asked forgiveness for all the hurts that I'd caused my kids, and others, by the choices I had made in my life.

For the first time, I confessed to Him that I knew it had been Him that day in the bathroom when I was fourteen. I thanked Him for saving my life then, and I asked for His help in the mess that I was now living. I asked for help to save my marriage. I had once again reached my breaking point, but this time I was calling out to Him.

CHAPTER NINE—FATHER'S LOVING HAND

It was during these months that, one night when I was back at home, I had a dream that was so vivid, so real, and came with instructions. That same evening I'd seen a friend of mine coming into the hospital as I was leaving work. I learned that she was coming to see her mother who was dying of cancer, and the family just waiting for her to slip away peacefully. That night I dreamt of this beautiful young woman who was twenty-three years old. In my dream, she was a beautiful angel hovering over her own funeral, smiling over all the people she could see who were there to celebrate her life.

I was sitting in a pew at the back of the church. I knew that it was my friend's mom's funeral because she was in the front row with her family and she was crying. I didn't know her mom personally, but I was at the funeral simply to pay my respects and support my friend. As I sat there, I could see her as this beautiful angel at the front of the chapel, facing outwards as she hovered and looked over the people, like she was so touched that they were there to honour her life. She was absorbing every moment of this precious memory into her very core.

The dress she wore was a beautiful shade of light pink, and her large and magnificent wings were soft-pillowy white, like nothing I'd ever seen before. As I sat in the pew looking up at her, I was awestruck to see her. I looked around, studying the people who were in attendance to see if anyone else was as awestruck as I, but no one else seemed to notice what I was seeing.

People were crying, bowing their heads and blowing their noses, but no one seemed to see what I was seeing. I said out loud, "Am I the only one who can see that?" People turned and looked at me like I was crazy, confused as to what I was referring.

My friend's mother answered my question by saying, "No one else can see me, Bonnie." I sat back in my pew, confused, awestruck, and bewildered. Then I woke up.

As I lay in my bed, quietly processing this vivid dream, I heard the same voice that I'd heard in the bathroom almost twenty years previously: "I want you to go to this woman in the hospital and tell her what you saw." I lay in bed, trying not to stir so as not to wake my husband.

I was bewildered, going over in my head all that I had seen in my dream, trying to determine just how I had seen this perfectly complete picture of a woman whom I'd never met, and trying to understand why she was twenty-three years old and not the elderly lady who I knew was lying in that hospital bed. And then there was the question of this voice. *Do I really do that? Do I really go there? People will think I'm nuts!*

When my husband woke up, I told him about the weird dream and explained the details to him. He replied in his sarcastic, mocking voice and with laughter in his tone: "Better not tell anyone about that one; everyone is sure to think you really are crazy ... if they don't already."

Okay, obviously telling him was a mistake, but this dream remained heavy on my heart, and it was like I could hear God's voice persisting that I follow through with what He'd asked me to do. For two weeks I went to and from work at the hospital, avoiding this persistent voice, and avoiding this woman's hospital room.

Finally one evening as I was driving home with my kids after their dance classes, I was overwhelmed with compulsion to obey this voice. He said, "Go now." Just after I crossed the railway tracks on the outskirts of town, I pulled my vehicle over to the side of the highway, pulled a U-turn, and headed back to the hospital, with my sweaty palms gripping the steering wheel. My kids asked what I was doing, and I explained that I'd forgotten something at work and had to run back for a minute.

When I arrived at the hospital, I told the kids to stay in the vehicle. I wasn't sure what I was going to tell the nursing staff, but I knew I had to go. As I came into the front entrance of the hospital, this woman's daughter walked around the corner and we met alone in the lobby. She was just leaving after visiting her mom. I was flustered and nervous beyond belief, but I tried to explain to her why I was there without having her think I was crazy.

Tears filled her eyes as I explained my dream to her, and that I was supposed to have come two weeks ago to tell her mother of my dream, but I didn't have the courage. I asked for her permission to go to her mother's room and talk with her. She was very touched that I would do that, and had no problem giving permission.

CHAPTER NINE—FATHER'S LOVING HAND

The nurses at the station had seen me talking with this woman, so I didn't have to explain why I was there. I simply said "Hi girls!" as I walked past and went directly to the mother's room.

When I arrived at her room, I sheepishly peeked around the corner before I entered. I was surprised to see a young man there. I wasn't expecting that, and I felt a little embarrassed as I then felt the need to explain to him why I was there. He said he was her son, and after I explained myself, he was very open to me speaking with his mom. He explained that she'd been unresponsive for days now, and he wasn't sure if she would hear me.

I acknowledged that, but told him that I had to deliver this message to her. He remained seated in his chair while I went over to the bed and took the woman's hand. I started talking to her, explaining who I was and that I'd come to give her a message. I explained in detail to her the dream that I'd had, and how I saw her as a beautiful twenty-three year old angel hovering over her own funeral. I explained everything I'd seen in my dream, said a quick prayer with her, and with tears in my eyes and a huge burden off my shoulders, I kissed her on the forehead and said, "Rest in peace now." It seemed to me that she smiled back.

I squeezed her hand and turned to leave. Her son looked up at me with tears in his eyes and managed to get out a whispered "Thank you." I walked out of the hospital, partly feeling elated for having fulfilled this task that had been given to me, and partly feeling embarrassed at this crazy thing that I'd just done.

It had been a leap for me. I'd had to trust this voice that I was hearing, this pressing on my heart that I felt, in order to follow through with what I'd been asked to do. It meant actually acknowledging that it wasn't just a dream. It meant risking looking like an idiot, and just believing.

As I drove home that night and then readied each of my kids for bed, I was in my own little world, immersed in thought about what had happened that night. I wouldn't tell anyone about that night for many years to come. It was like that moment in time was my pearls, too precious to give away to just anyone. The very next day, I found out that the woman had passed away peacefully just hours after I'd left her hospital room. What was this thing that was happening to me?

***

My time in the convent (ha-ha … not many people can say this) completely changed me. Something was happening in the very core of me, and it was happening irrevocably. I started to feel this peace in me; this connection to God became more and more tangible. And it was something that I was very inexperienced at.

Naturally, my soul started yearning for more of this "connection," so I started seeking out a place where I'd feel comfortable exploring these spiritual things that were fairly new to me. I knew a woman who often talked about this "connection" she had with God, and how she talked to spirits. Out of curiosity, I started going to her meditation classes. I was on this really great path towards inner peace and inner healing, even though there were things about her classes that I thought were just plain weird. As she would ready herself to lead us into a new meditation/yoga pose, she'd say, "Remember I always say, take what you want and leave the rest. We all need a connection to a higher power, and we all need to feel rooted, but we don't have to accept anything that is not comfortable either."

Okay, I thought, *I can live with that.* The only thing about spiritual things that I really knew for sure was that there was no denying there really was a God. As far as I could tell, this meditation thing, where we were getting in touch with God and our inner selves, seemed like a pretty good thing. I was really searching for God, and I was beginning to see why people were drawn here—freedom from "religious law" and increasing my own inner healing and peace.

I began to spend more and more time in this woman's classes and at her wholeness and healing spa. One time I went for a massage and she talked to me about meditation and talking with "spirits." I told her something that I hadn't really told anyone else—that even though I was thankful for the time I'd spend at the convent, sometimes it was really eerie staying there.

She explained to me that it was no secret that bad spirits existed; she saw them all the time, so she walked me through how to meditate out bad spirits. The thought of it scared me, but I was naïve and soaked in every word of teaching and advice. I was soon to learn the dangers of messing with the spiritual realm without the protection of the Holy Spirit, and Jesus would once again come to my rescue.

One night when I was lying in my bed at the convent, I felt this darkness all around me. I can't really explain it, but I felt darkness and heaviness. I started meditating, like I'd been instructed. The doorway to my room was on my right side, just on the other side of the bedside table, at the head of my bed. As I was lying there with my eyes closed, I suddenly saw a dark shadow, like a black silhouette, standing in the doorway of my room. I could feel my heartbeat quicken in my chest; my breathing became panicked as I tried to slow and control it without making a sound. I was unsure of what to do or really what was happening.

As I lay there with my eyes closed, I could then see two little boys in my room, one in each corner of the room on the left side of my bed. They were both huddled in the fetal position, rocking back and forth like they were scared. Somehow I knew that these two little boys were afraid of the dark shadow in the doorway.

I was scared. I could tell by the pounding in my chest that this was really happening, and my logical brain was trying to wrap itself around what was happening and what I should do next. Then suddenly, on the wall at the foot of my bed, appeared Jesus. He was sitting on a small stump with His arms wide open and His long, white robe draped over his lap to his feet. I could see a short ladder on the wall just below Him, which obviously was the way up.

He said to me, "Bonnie, you tell those two little boys to come and sit on my knee."

It appeared that the boys could also hear Him, because when I said to the boys, "It's okay, you can go and sit. It's Jesus," there was no hesitation from the first little boy, who got up from the corner of the room and went over to the short ladder, climbed up, and sat on His knee.

As soon as the boy sat down on Jesus' knee, I could feel this breath of healing, a release, a freedom that filled the room. It was instantaneous. I actually remember thinking to myself, *Some grown man has just been healed.*

The second little boy was too afraid to go. I went over to him and said, "It's okay. You will be safe there." I went over to him and encouraged him to get up. He went over to the ladder, and I boosted him up.

By this time, the first little boy was skipping circles around Jesus; he was like a young boy skipping and celebrating the innocence of childhood, freed from the bonds of hurt, pain, and fear.

The second little boy timidly approached Jesus, and as soon as he sat on Jesus' knee, I felt the same thing again. This breath of healing that filled the room, like a gentle breeze coming through the window that filled each corner of the room. It was pure, peaceful, saturating.

In the same moment that the second little boy sat on Jesus' knee and the breath of healing came over the room, the dark shadow in the doorway beside me disappeared in an instant. The heaviness was gone; the darkness, gone; the fear, gone.

I lay there with my eyes still closed and tears streaming down my face, wondering what had just happened. My logical self tried to process it, but it was like a wave of emotion and an experience that I couldn't quite grasp.

As I lay there wondering what the purpose of all this was, Jesus said this to me: "Okay, Bonnie, it's your turn." The words were like a bolt of lightening going through my body. I was completely taken aback, and I lost control of my emotions. I started sobbing, and the tears streamed uncontrollably down my face. Logically, I wasn't really sure what to do. Here I was lying in bed with my eyes closed, seeing all of this and trying to wrap my brain around what I was supposed to do. All of a sudden, involuntarily, I watched as my five year old little self—that same little girl who walked home from the haunted house that day in October of 1975—I watched her rise up out of my body and go and sit on Jesus' knee.

> The healing was instant and complete. I felt this incredible release, like a washing of peace over me. The shame and the rage that once saturated me to the core were gone; the void I'd spent my whole life trying to satisfy was filled, refreshed from a spring of living water.

CHAPTER NINE—FATHER'S LOVING HAND

The healing was instant and complete. I felt this incredible release, like a washing of peace over me. The shame and the rage that once saturated me to the core were gone; the void I'd spent my whole life trying to satisfy was filled, refreshed from a spring of living water. In an instant I was whole, complete, healed, made new.

I faded off to sleep that night, wrapped in a sense of awe and wonder over what I'd experienced. I slept deeply, like never before, like I was curled up in the palm of the Almighty God Himself.

Bruce's song: "Father's Loving Hand"

Chapter Ten

METAMORPHOSIS ... AND THE FLY

You cannot experience the healing touch of Jesus and ever be the same again. The anger and rage that once consumed my being were gone; the shame that I felt so deep within was gone. Like a slate, I was wiped clean. I felt a freedom from who I used to be, like a freshness that I couldn't explain, and I felt it to the very core of my being. I would later understand that what I had experienced was a vision. That weekend, I didn't know what it was—I just knew that it was undeniable, and something told me that it was a new dawning.

As I drove home, I was overjoyed thinking about all that had transpired over the weekend in me. I had such a freedom in my spirit, I actually thought, *This is going to save my marriage!* I had such peace in me, I literally felt new. *This must be what people mean when they talk about the grace and forgiveness of Jesus.* I knew it would change everything ... and that it did.

The day after I got home from the convent, I was feeling so ecstatic that I felt drawn to go to my favourite décor store in town to find a plaque, a picture, or something that would capture what I'd experienced—a keepsake that would help me savour that moment in my life.

The store had many inspiring wall hangings and figurines that reflected hope and faith, so I felt sure I'd find something there. When I opened the front door of the store, I looked down to make sure I didn't miss the step up. As I had my feet firmly planted upon the step, I looked up as I entered through the door. My attention was immediately drawn up to a large, new picture that was hanging high on the east wall.

My mouth dropped to the floor, my eyes welled up with tears, and my whole body tingled the moment I saw it. I was speechless. It was me as a little girl! The woman who owned the store, a friend of mine, witnessed my reaction as I came in the door.

"Isn't she beautiful," she said. "I just got her in over the weekend."

I stood there in awe. It looked exactly like the little girl I was when I was five, except this one had soft, feathery wings that came out from behind her, the same kind of wings that I had seen in my dream of my friend's mom.

Trying to contain my emotion, I explained to her, "It's me! I actually have a photo of me when I was five that's identical to that picture. It's me!" She had no idea what I was talking about, but I knew that I had to have that portrait. I knew that God was giving me this tangible gift to remind me of what had happened to me that weekend at the convent, so that I'd never forget what He did for me, how He redeemed me and made me new.

When I got home that same day, I dug through my childhood photos and found the photo that I knew I had. It was almost identical to the portrait. It truly was me. As I studied the small photo and the stamp on the back, I realized the most amazing thing—this photo had been taken in September 1975, exactly one month before my haunted house experience. This meant that the little girl in the photo still had her childhood innocence, her purity, and a whole spirit. Through the miracle of the weekend, and through the healing touch of Jesus, this little girl had been restored in me, whole and complete again. I sat on the living room floor, sobbing with a grateful heart to the Lord for this amazing gift.

All of these things I would keep in my heart and secret place for many months to come, and I would tell only a select few of my experiences. Because of his reaction to my dream of the angel at her own funeral, I never did tell my husband what happened to me at the convent, but I was so excited about the changes in my life. I knew the change in me

CHAPTER TEN—METAMORPHOSIS...AND THE FLY

was real; I could feel it in the way I spoke to my husband. I could feel it in the way I dealt with my kids, I felt it in my confidence at work, and I felt this continuing peace in my being. It was like something that was unshakeable.

***

When I had driven home that weekend, I knew that what had happened to me would change everything. I didn't, however, anticipate the changes to end up the way they did. I really thought that this was the shift that would save my marriage. To the core of my being I didn't feel the deep anger or rage in me, or the desire to fight with him anymore.

I guess the best way to describe it is that I changed the game, and he didn't like it. We had already established such a pattern of violence and volatile behaviour that my unwillingness to fight back didn't calm his anger as I'd expected it would; it only made him crazier that he couldn't get me to react anymore. His anger not only escalated in the months to follow, but his cruel words became relentless, and the physical abuse bordered on "out of control."

To put all the blame on him would be wrong; together we had established this volatile pattern of behaviour in our home, and it was really all we knew. I imagine that it probably did make him crazy that I wouldn't fight back, but I couldn't help the change in my heart, and I wasn't about to enter back in to the darkness.

Regardless, the abuse in our home escalated until we reached that "night of terror" in late September which would mark the end of our marriage. That night is probably the most traumatic incident that my kids will ever experience in their lives. It has left deep wounds in each one of them—wounds that God has, and will, continue to heal in His time.

***

So now I found myself on my own again. As I began my new life with my three young girls, this new faith that was growing in me was creating changes in me, like a metamorphosis of my entire being. I have never been a person to take things one cautious step at a time. It's all or nothing with

> If there's one thing I've learned in this life of faith, it's that if God has a plan for it, He will always work out the details.

me, and I've only ever had one gear … full-speed ahead! God must've been shaking His head knowing the task He had ahead of Him, trying to reign me in!

Even though I was a "baby Christian," He began to show me what a life of abandoned faith looks like. I gradually became so thirsty to hear Him that I would spend hours on my knees, praying and seeking Him. As He led, I began to see Him in even the smallest of things.

If there's one thing I've learned in this life of faith, it's that if God has a plan for it, He will always work out the details. In the months to come, He would begin to make His plan for me clear.

***

A few years prior to our "night of terror," my oldest daughter, J, who would have been going on thirteen years old at the time, met Jesus at summer camp. She really struggled with bullying in the public school in the small town where we lived, and since her summer camp experience, she'd been asking if she could go to a private Christian boarding school in a small town in Saskatchewan.

My husband's answer was a definite "No." Although I could see that she needed some kind of hope and relief from the constant fighting at home, and the constant bullying she experienced at school, I couldn't imagine sending her away from our family.

Now here it was a couple of years later, in early spring, after I'd been on my own with the girls for a number of months, and J's heart continued to be at boarding school, and she continued to press me for permission. I told her that I just couldn't see how I could send her away with my responsibilities to my regular day-time ambulance and hospital maintenance hours, not to mention my on-call hours, which basically kept me bound to my job 24/7. I needed her to be home if my radio went off, and I couldn't see how it would ever work for her to go away to boarding school. "But," I said, "I will pray about it." Something I've learned that you should never do unless you're willing to let the wrenches fly!

CHAPTER TEN—METAMORPHOSIS...AND THE FLY

One Sunday morning, I sent the girls into their early morning Sunday school classes. Rather than going to my adult Sunday school class, I went into the chapel where I could be on my knees and alone with God. As I laid out my dilemma before God, asking His guidance for my decision regarding J, I was repeatedly distracted by a fly that kept making a strange kind of buzzing noise on the step in front of where I was kneeling.

Intrigued, I started watching the fly, who kept walking in circles and then would go to the edge of the step, only to pace around in another circle. As I studied the fly more carefully, I realized that his wings were partly stuck to his back and he couldn't fly. It was an epiphany for me! God spoke to me in that moment, and I answered aloud with "ah ha" in my voice: "She can't fly! I get it! She can't fly!"

As soon as I made that connection and got the message God was trying to send me, the fly walked to the edge of the step, ruffled its wings, and flew off towards the light of the window! I sat there utterly amazed at the private little experience I'd just had with God and that fly, and I knew what I had to do.

As we sat around the lunch table that day after church, I tried to be very calm and collected, even though I was bursting with excitement to tell J the great news! I still wasn't sure how it was all going to work, because I knew I'd be on call 24/7, and the question still remained as to what I would do in the middle of the night if I had to leave on a call and she wasn't home. But I also knew that God was telling me this was the right thing for her, so I had to trust that He would figure out the details.

J was ecstatic with the news. Relief came in the tears that flowed ... tears of joy. It was just the hope she needed to help get her through the spring term at school in our small town. She would be starting her Grade 10 year in a private Christian high school, with new Christian friends.

Over the next number of months, God began to lay on my heart that we should all be moving to this quaint little town with J. Despite what I felt God was laying on my heart, there were huge obstacles that were standing in the way, and none of it made any sense to me, so I didn't see how any of it would be possible.

Besides, I absolutely loved our new home, and I was proud of it! Owning it was very liberating for me. I wasn't able only to afford our home, but a new vehicle as well, all on my own! In addition, I absolutely loved my job, and I couldn't imagine leaving it. I had finally reached my goal of becoming a Primary Care Paramedic, and I was not about to give that up either. On top of that, I was in the middle of a custody battle, and so far had more than ten thousand dollars in legal bills! Besides, there was no way that anybody would be moving into this small town in Saskatchewan who would pay what I needed to get out of my new house.

Knowing the odds were in my favour, and being sure that I would come out on top, I made a deal with God. I told Him that if He removed all of the obstacles, which seemed insurmountable to me, then I would go, for whatever purpose He had. And I left it at that.

One thing is sure—if you ever decide to make a deal with God and give Him the authority to "handle your affairs," you better be ready and willing for the Lion of Judah to arise in your life! Within weeks of my deal-making with God, things started to move in my ex-husband's court case. He had been charged by the RCMP with spousal assault, and the Crown Prosecutor was eager to try his case. I received a call from the Crown Prosecutor one day, saying that he was confused as to how this happened, because usually court appearances can be delayed up to months, but for some reason, our case had been bumped up and would be heard much sooner than we'd anticipated.

Because my ex-husband was pleading not guilty, the Crown Prosecutor had to call my two older children as witnesses, something he'd normally avoid at all cost so that they wouldn't have to live through the trauma again. Now with the trial being bumped up, the Crown was concerned about the girls and was calling to make sure we were ready, as it was coming very fast.

We were ready, and my girls bravely faced everyone in the courtroom, speaking directly to the judge as they had been instructed, despite the fiery looks and gasps of disbelief that my ex-husband's family tried to intimidate them with. At the end of it all, my husband was convicted by his own confession, but certainly not one he gave in court under oath.

CHAPTER TEN—METAMORPHOSIS...AND THE FLY

In his own way of processing the big fight we'd had that cold night in September, my husband confessed to his friend the very next day: "I don't know what happened to me, man. I just went crazy, and I was throwing her around the yard like a rag doll."

In presenting their case, the defense smugly called witnesses to defame my character as best they could—this young man being one of them. But in the end, the Crown Prosecutor poked a huge hole in the defense's case when he asked this particular witness a simple question: "Did the defendant say these words to you the day after the events of that September evening: 'I don't know what happened to me, man. I just went crazy, and I was throwing her around the yard like a rag doll.'"

Being a man of integrity, his only answer could be "Yes." Guilty verdict ... case closed. Custody became a non-issue; in fact, the judge ruled that my husband would not be allowed to see his daughter for an entire year, unless I consented. Obstacle one, out of the way.

As the pieces started falling together, I decided I had better go to this place and check it out. If we were to move there, I would surely need a job and a home. I had no luck getting a job. I applied everywhere in town, on campus, and in the surrounding area. Each initial meeting or interview came up empty. After two return trips to try and land myself some security for my kids, I began to doubt that this was what I was supposed to be doing, so I went back to my knees to ask God if maybe I'd gotten it wrong.

This is what I heard Him say to me: "Bonnie, think about what's in the town where I'm sending you." As I was kneeling at the side of my bed, I sat up on the backs of my calves, intently trying to consider this. Then it hit me.

"School?" I said out loud in my conversation with God. "You're sending me to school?" As I sat there dumbfounded, I exclaimed, "You want me to go to school! Like ministry school?"

Pondering to myself how this could ever be possible, I felt relief and a huge weight lifted off my shoulders. I just felt an overwhelming peace. "Wow!" I said out loud as I sat there dumbfounded.

I came running out of my room to tell the girls this new revelation. "Girls! I've figured it out! I can't find a job because I'm not supposed to go there to work; I'm supposed to go to school!" It all made complete sense now, and I wondered how I didn't see it before.

I started to let myself get excited at the possibility of moving to a new community with a fresh start, but there were still some things tugging at my heart. I really loved my house, and each time I walked into the living room, I looked around at the way I'd decorated and painted, and I mourned a little at the thought of not living here. I loved the hand-painted verses on the wall, and my custom-made blinds and silk drapes, and it broke my heart to think of having to leave.

Then there was my job. Oh how I loved my job! I'd worked so hard to become a Primary Care Paramedic. I believe God knew how difficult it would be for me to give up my job, so I guess He figured lessening my options would help me make up my mind. It was then that I had my treacherous, yet miraculous, horse wreck that would completely take me out of commission and bring me to a place in my heart where I knew I was of no use to anyone but Him, so I may as well give up the reigns.

It would also be in my hospital bed a few days after that horse wreck where I would receive a phone call—on the hospital phone of all things—from a teacher who was going to be new to town, had heard that my house may be for sale, and was willing to pay whatever I was asking for my house, even though it wasn't officially up for sale yet and she hadn't seen it!

Interestingly enough, I made enough money from that house deal to pay off my legal bill completely and to pay cash for a house trailer in this quaint little town, with enough money left over to add on two bedrooms and an office. It seemed in the end that God was the one who had the upper hand in His arrangement with me, and I was astounded at how He removed each humungous obstacle that I had laid out before Him, like they were mere sticks in His path.

Metamorphosis was happening in me. There was an irrevocable change that was happening. I was beginning to realize that the God who gifted me this life actually had a plan for me. But it would be for His purposes, not mine.

Bruce's song: "Reach"

Chapter Eleven

SPREADING MY WINGS

Breaking family secrets that keep you bound in shame is kind of like removing a sliver that festers. This is exactly where I found myself the summer before Jesus met me at the convent. Our family, on my mom's side, had planned a large family reunion, but I'd reached a point where I couldn't bring myself to attend another family gathering and pretend that I was having a great time with my cousin lurking in the background and me, now a grown woman, being on edge the entire weekend to ensure that he stayed free and clear of me and my children.

In order to find freedom from the bondage of the shame, I could see that my only option was to risk becoming the black sheep of the family, take the plunge over the cliff, and "spill the beans" on my cousin's secret game that he'd forced me to play as a child. Some will say I did this bravely, and others will say I did it selfishly to cause division. No matter what anyone says, I'd do it all over again, because it was the beginning of my journey of healing.

The relief of getting that sliver out was incredibly liberating for me, and in the process, I discovered that as long as the sliver remains hidden under the surface, it causes infection that no one can see. I also discovered that sometimes the sliver has been there so long, covered up with so many different salves, that you have to fight and dig to get it out, even hurting the surrounding tissue. But as soon as you remove it, deliverance from the pain takes place, and the healing can begin—that is, if you choose not to cover it up again.

I chose to not pretend anymore, but to come out from under the curse of this shame that was so deeply entrenched in me from childhood. I chose to let my wounds air in the openness. This resulted not only in healing for me, but for others who, unbeknownst to me, had suffered similar experiences. They were, by their own choice, also freed of the shame that bound them to our family secrets, which apparently ran deeper than any of us knew. It wasn't just me! How liberating this was for me!

Of course, many chose (and still choose) to ostracize me, kind of like a convenient "blame the victim" scenario. Others choose to stay in the background, entrenched in their own deeper secrets for whatever reason. Regardless, the secrets that kept me bound were now broken, and I was on my own journey of healing.

I believe it was because I'd been seeking freedom from this shame and pain for so long that God was able to get a hold of my life the way He did. I was like dry bones, eager to be filled with fresh sinew, clean flesh, and new life! The freedom from the bondage of family secrets made it possible for me to turn to God, and when I turned to face Him, I realized He'd been there all along, ready to receive me in a mighty way.

As I'd come to this leg in my journey, I came to realize that all the things I tried to fill my life with, such as drinking, drugs, men, self-help feel-good remedies, and empty spiritual paths, would never have given me the whole and complete healing that I'd found in Jesus. I was free, and I was sold-out for Him, for the One who had saved me; I was ready to give my all for Him. So it was now, without obstacle, that my girls and I made our big move to begin a new chapter.

***

The thought of Bible college intimidated me. Up until that point, I'd hardly even opened my Bible. I was a "baby Christian," and I knew that I was in WAY over my head. I also knew that I was doing exactly what I was called to do, and somehow God would see me through.

CHAPTER ELEVEN—SPREADING MY WINGS

I was anticipating the upcoming changes in our lives and awaiting the end of the school year for my girls so that we'd be free to move. A few days before our move, I wrote this in my journal: "I feel like the last piece of the puzzle of the first half of my life has been placed." I was now ready to begin my life … my new life. It was like I'd just been born into a whole new being, in a whole new measure of life. It was scary, but way more exhilarating than scary!

On moving day, we arrived with our big moving truck. Much to my surprise and amazement, people started coming from out of the woodwork to help us unload. Neighbours, people passing by, all perfect strangers came to help us unload our truck. As we made trips back and forth from the moving truck to the house, I started a conversation with a young woman who had come to help. She questioned why I was registered in the college and not the seminary. Puzzled, I asked her, "What's seminary?"

Scratching her head, she very graciously replied, "Um, we need to talk."

I still thank God for sending her that day and for her ability to patiently accept my incredible naivety. As I would find out, seminary was for either "mature" students or people with an undergraduate degree who were studying to earn a Masters Degree in their choice of ministry. I didn't have an undergraduate degree, so I'd only qualify for the seminary if I was a "mature" student, meaning I had to be thirty-five years old by September 1. As it would happen, I'd be turning thirty-five on August 30 of that year! Mmm … coincidence? Upon hearing my story, the registrar gave me a resounding "YES" to enter the seminary as opposed to the college. Thus would begin the hardest three years of my life.

***

My first modular class was called Pentateuch. Really? I had to confide in my fifteen year old daughter that I didn't know what "Pentateuch" meant. Shaking her head at the obvious hopelessness of my case, she informed me that it was the first five books of the Bible. Okay then, now I had a place to start!

I was greener than green when I entered seminary in September, 2005, but I had God's favour, some very patient professors, and some really incredible friends who supported me. When I started my program in Youth and Family Ministry, I was told that because I didn't have an undergraduate degree in Social Work, I'd only qualify to receive a Certificate of the Seminary. There was a loophole however—I could go on to achieve a Masters degree if, half-way through my program, I had a good GPA, had fulfilled all of the academic requirements to date, and had the full backing of the entire seminary faculty. I was told this was unlikely, due to my lack of biblical knowledge and background, but for me, a certificate would just not do. I had my mind on that Masters degree before I even entered my first classroom, and I would not be swayed.

The professor in charge of my Youth and Family Ministry program often described my experiences in seminary as drinking from a fire hydrant. It wasn't unusual for me to be sitting across from his desk, using all the tissues in his Kleenex box, as he patiently tried to keep me on course and encourage me to keep persevering. Often our conversations centred on him trying to help me realize that I was not a race-horse that should just run with every thought, impression, or word from God. More often than I can even remember, his words to me were, "Bonnie, you have to learn that you are not a thoroughbred that just runs. You have to give God the reins; let Him bridle you in."

On top of all the modular classes, the reading, the pre-work and post-work for my classes, I was also a single mom of three vastly diverse girls who had just come out of an immensely difficult life crisis. I was a "baby Christian" learning all of the "politically correct" ways of living in a Christian community, and my whole being was being transformed from the inside-out. And now I was supposed to learn how to canter at the Lord's pace too?

Learning how to be a "good Christian" in this "perfect" little community was one of the more difficult tasks I'd face. "Oh … you people don't smoke?" Okay, guess I better keep that hidden in my back yard. "Oh … you people don't yell at your kids?" Guess I better tone that one down too! "Oh … you people don't swear?" Yikes! I am in trouble! "Oh … you think that I was wrong to divorce my husband, and I'll never be allowed to remarry?" Oh my! The shame of it! What am I to do now? "Oh … I am a woman, so I'm not supposed to become a pastor. I should consider counselling?" I'm confused. Why does this matter? There is so much to learn about how to be a good Christian! "I guess by all the looks that I get in the hallways and on the streets of this little town, I'm not doing such a great job so far?"

"How does one possibly measure up to you people? How am I to fit in your box? How could I possibly think that I'd be accepted into a Christian community? That I could ever measure up to calling myself a Christian? That I could ever become a pastor? This is actually not what I was expecting when God sent me for a fresh start in a new community … of Christian people. You are all Christian, aren't you? Cause … something isn't making sense to me. I've met this man named Jesus that you all keep talking about, and He is nothing like this!"

***

These, however, would not be the hardest lessons I'd have to learn during my time in seminary. God didn't waste any time teaching me obedience, heeding His voice, and having courage to abide in Him alone … no matter what any man would have to say about it.

In November of 2005, during my first semester of seminary, He started waking me in the night. Sometimes I'd hear a knock at the door, even though no one was there; sometimes I'd hear the phone or the doorbell, and I knew it was Him waking me to spend time with Him. Sometimes, He'd just wake me out of a dead sleep and tell me to get up, get on my knees, and pray for someone specific. This was a whole new learning paradigm, and the greatest lesson would be that my fear of God must always be greater that my fear of man. My fears of what they will do or say cannot stop me from being obedient to what God is asking of me. These would not be easy lessons for this young single mom, a woman in ministry of all things, divorced three times!

God told me that I must learn to pray through everything, and He would teach me how. I created a prayer corner in my room where I'd spend most of my early mornings on my knees, seeking His will, His guidance, and His teaching. Often it was like we were having a face-to-face conversation. Being on my knees in my prayer corner was simply a discipline that I knew I had to be diligent at.

When I wasn't diligent and committed to it, things in my life became really hard. I would drift further from the Lord, and His provision of gifts such as self-control, peace, joy, love, patience, discernment, obedience, and courage would be far from my being. But when I was diligent and committed to it, He strengthened me to walk through anything.

Countless mornings, God would wake me with, "Come, spend time with me. Come, I have something to tell you." He would speak into my spirit. I was emotionally and physically exhausted, yet He was persistent in waking me, teaching me obedience.

There was so much for me to learn. Each class that I took, each assignment, each paper, I knew there were things for me to learn in even the smallest of tasks. I made a habit of praying through each assignment, and He told me which paper topic I should choose, where to find my research, and what He wanted me to learn in each one.

He was teaching me not only how to know His Word, but how He had every answer for every question necessary for a life in Him. He was teaching me how to be bold in my faith, how to listen only to His voice, how to be obedient, how to forgive those who had hurt me, how to pray for those same people and live in the freedom of His grace, how to intercede for others, and how to be broken bread and poured out wine for Him.

No doubt there were people that God sent along my path to help me through this time. After experiencing some of the difficulties of learning to live out my faith in a community of "politically correct Christians," He sent me some mentors to help me learn how to discern, how to seek God for confirmations of what He was asking, and how to follow through in obedience when I knew for sure what I was to do. Their support, encouragement, and teaching have been invaluable to me, even in my life today as I seek to do God's will in every decision I make. The greatest lesson they taught me was not to go ahead of God, and not to "connect the dots" myself.

Sometimes we think God is saying one thing, but we maybe don't have the full picture. It's easy then to connect the dots and conclude that we know what He's speaking about. Acting on my own conclusions has proven to be detrimental in some cases, but it's all part of the learning process.

My mentors taught me that when I feel God is laying something on my heart, pressing it into my very being, then I am to pray and wait for three confirmations before I go ahead. One of these confirmations must be from the Word, so I have an extra measure of confidence that it is the Lord leading.

This rule of self-discipline has been vital to me for making both big and small decisions as I seek to live out my life for the Lord. It has helped develop and mature my spiritual gifts so that I am better able to serve the Lord in the way He is calling me. It has disciplined me to be in the Word every day of my life, seeking in ALL things His direction. It has bridled me to keep me from going ahead of the Lord's time. Mostly, it has taught me that we have a living God! The same God that parted the sea for the Israelites to cross in safety on dry ground is the same God that cares about and directs me in every decision I make in life.

***

With the support of my mentors, and the new lessons I was learning, I seemed to be sailing through seminary with the favour of the Lord. By October of 2006, just into my second year, I was called in for a seminary review. My GPA was a high 3 out of 4, and I had the full backing of the seminary faculty to continue in my studies and work towards a Masters degree, even though I didn't have an undergraduate degree. Though there were many hard lessons, God gave me the strength to walk with my head high, with His courage and confidence, and in His favour.

The Lord continued to wake me in the wee hours of the morning and lay things upon my heart. I steadily learned, sometimes through mistakes, how to respond to the things He was showing me. I was passionate, steadfast, and tenacious when it came to my faith, as well as my schooling. There were some, though, who couldn't get past the fact that I was a woman in ministry, better yet a multiple-divorced woman in ministry, and so bold in my faith. This would prove to be a real challenge for me in my last half of seminary, one that would almost break me.

One day as our church was in search for a new pastor, the Lord told me in church to stand up and speak these words: "As you search for a new pastor, the Lord wants you to know this: 'The Lord wants unity in our community.'" I sat there in my chair arguing with God, telling Him that I was not going to do this! I said to Him, "I can't do this unless you give me three confirmations."

Involuntarily, the next thing I knew I was standing and those same words were coming out of my mouth. I wasn't sure what to think. I knew there would be repercussions, and some who would look down their noses at me. I knew this would surely be something that we discussed at my next meeting with my mentors, but I also knew that it wasn't me who picked me up out of that chair and spoke those words.

As I expected, the very next day I was called into the office of a seminary professor with whom I didn't really have that much to do. He was the head of a different program than mine, so we didn't know each other well. He sat me in his office and proceeded to tell me that I had better be careful during the rest of my time in seminary. "I believe you are being used by Satan," he said, "because you are so immature in your faith." Wow. What does one do with that kind of assault? I left his office extremely discouraged and embarrassed.

On my walk home, I was bombarded with overwhelming thoughts and questions: *Is this what they think of me? I'm just trying to learn how to be obedient here, and you tell me I'm being used by Satan! How can you even think that? You don't even know who I am, let alone my walk with God. How am I to learn and grow under such criticism? Why don't you come alongside me then, and teach me how to do this thing called faith?*

It was a very discouraging time for me, and I could feel my tenacious spirit beginning to crumble. Though I felt I was under constant criticism by some, the Lord continued to wake me and give me direction and guidance in the early morning hours.

Seminary chapel was a smaller, more intimate stetting than the large college chapel. One week, the Lord gave me a burden to pray for a couple in our community who were struggling. It wasn't a secret that this family was struggling, as they themselves had sent out prayer requests to the larger community. During seminary chapel, I stood and shared this burden that the Lord had given me, and asked if the men could break off and pray for the man, and if the women could break off and pray for the woman.

Again, the very next day, I was called into the office of another professor, one whom I knew even less than the first one who reprimanded me for speaking out in church. He had also brought along a fellow student of mine who was involved in the planning of our seminary chapels. I was told by the two of them that it was inappropriate for me to speak out in chapel and ask for intercessory prayer for this couple, that I was spiritually immature, and that I was to never speak out in chapel again.

A few weeks after this incident, I went to my rented study carrel in the library, where I kept all of my books and research to work on during the week. I found a book lying in the centre of my desk that had been placed there very carefully by someone. It was titled, *Only Men Belong in Leadership*. I sat there lost in my own discouraging thoughts. *Who even writes a book like this, let alone leaves it on the desk of a woman who is studying in a Christian seminary? Whatever happened to building each other up in the faith?* Nevertheless, it was another fiery arrow that pierced my heart, one of many that seemed to be relentlessly coming my way as I tried to persevere in this task of getting my Masters degree.

It would be only weeks after the "book" incident that I would be preparing for my first mission trip to Mexico. I was the student leader, and part of my practicum responsibilities were to help plan and facilitate this trip. However, in the weeks leading up to the trip, I would find myself in the middle of a very controversial situation. A woman I knew had come to me and confided that she and her husband were going through a terrible separation. She'd been looking forward to the upcoming Easter holidays to spend some quality time with her kids at her parents' home, but her husband had gone behind her back and made arrangements for her kids to go on the Mexico trip with him, leaving her alone for the Easter holidays. She was completely broken and distraught about the situation, and knowing my history of abuse and the fact that I had played a large part in the planning of this trip, she had come to me for advice.

I went to the person in charge of the mission trip and explained how the arrangements for the man's children to go with us had been manipulated by the father. He seemed unaware of the situation, and I left it in his hands to deal with. A week later, the mother of the children came to me distraught again, because nothing had been done.

Dissatisfied with the lack of response and the lack of acknowledgement of the injustice in the situation, I went to an elder of the church and explained the situation. I explained, as I had to the person in charge, that if I was to help supervise this mission trip, I wasn't comfortable accompanying children without the consent of the mother. I expressed that it would be like kidnapping, and I felt strongly that something needed to be done. I left it in the hands of the elder, and he assured me they would handle it uprightly.

From there, I walked to the post office to pick up my mail, and happened to meet the father of the children along my path. It was awkward, because he knew that I had spoken up about the situation, but I was not intimidated by him and I asked him if we could talk. I explained to him that I didn't want any animosity between the two of us, but that I felt what he did was not right. I assured him that I didn't judge him, but that I was standing up for what I thought was right, and I would've done the same for him if the tables had been turned. I explained to him that I didn't want to be in the middle, and it was out of my hands at this point, but I hoped we could get along on the trip for the sake of the high school kids going with us, if nothing else.

He agreed it was important that we get along for that reason, and that was the end of our conversation. The church handled the situation in a way that was suitable to the couple. I felt relief, and put the situation out of my mind.

The days went on, and the anticipation of our trip became more and more real. I couldn't wait to get to Mexico and meet all those little ones to whom we'd spread a little love for the time we were there! The night before our departure, I was busy packing, ensuring that J had all of her stuff together for the time that she'd be away with the tour choir, helping D get packed for spending the Easter with Grandma and Grandpa, and

CHAPTER ELEVEN—SPREADING MY WINGS

spending every precious minute with R before she'd be sent to her dad's place for the Easter break. In the middle of my busyness, I received a phone call from the person in charge of the mission trip, asking if I could come to his office. *Umm, do you forget the fact that I am a single mom and have not only myself, but three girls, to get ready for the two weeks that I'm to be away?* I thought.

I was annoyed, but agreed to meet with him. Obviously, there were last minute plans that we'd overlooked, and we needed to take care of them. When I walked into his office, he was sitting there with another female supervisor who was also coming along with us.

He couldn't really explain the reasons, other than saying, "I just don't think it's going to work for you to come, and it would be better if you stayed home."

Shocked and completely in disbelief, I had to hear it again, so I asked, "Are you asking me to stay home?"

He said he thought it was best.

I left his office utterly confused, dumbfounded, and hurt beyond words. They couldn't give me a definite reason why they were asking me to stay behind from a mission trip that I had helped plan … just that they thought it was better. I felt like I'd just been blindsided without warning. *How humiliating*, I thought as I stumbled home, bellowing in tears that night. *What about all of those kids whose lives I speak into, who will be loading that bus tomorrow morning wondering where I am? What am I to say to them? What will they say to them?* I hardly slept a wink that night. I wept bitterly all through the night, wondering what I could've possibly done to deserve such harsh treatment.

Thoughts went through my mind all night: *Did I not participate enough in the planning? Did I not do a good job? Maybe I messed something up really badly? Could it possibly have anything to do with this situation that I had spoken up about weeks ago?*

I would spend days and weeks trying to pick myself up from this one; it was almost like being hit by a semi truck. I literally felt flattened—emotionally, mentally, spiritually, and physically.

***

Through all of these trials, the Lord found creative ways to keep me encouraged. Many times I would go to my study carrel in the library and find a note from one of my kids, encouraging me and telling me how much they loved me, or how proud of me they were. I had a couple of close friends who really "got me" that I could always count on for a shoulder to cry on. I also volunteered at the Fire Department, just so that I could get my "adrenaline fix." It was a good outlet for me. It helped me keep my paramedic blood flowing, and it helped them out with a first responder.

I was a single mom, and my student loan didn't cover a lot of expenses. Occasionally, I'd be met at the door with bags or baskets of groceries. Randomly, people would drop off things for our family, and always at the most crucial of times.

There were times of incredible blessing and abundance too. One December, the Lord sent an anonymous gift of $10,000.00 to my doorway four days before Christmas! That would be the beginning of God teaching me to rely on Him alone … for everything. The following year, I received a car for my birthday. Many things the Lord did to keep me encouraged through this time … miracles, really.

In my second year, I was asked to serve as the chaplain for the girls' hockey team, which was an honour for me. Those girls became like daughters to me. Sometimes some of my hockey girls would leave notes of encouragement too, and they always did crazy things to let me know how much I was appreciated. The high school girls whom I mentored one on one also encouraged me. There were always plenty of hugs for me in the hallways, and it was what the Lord knew I needed to stay encouraged.

During my last summer in seminary, I was given my choice of summer camps by the director of the Canadian Sunday School Mission to fill the role of Spiritual Director to the staff in the upcoming summer season. It was a new position he'd created specifically for me, and it was incredibly affirming to me that someone thought that highly of me to offer me such an honour. All of these encouraging experiences helped balance the scales for me between trial and blessing.

The Lord always knew exactly what I needed, and He'd often send someone right into my path to encourage me. As I walked home from school one day, I was particularly discouraged. I met a woman on the road whom I didn't know well, but she lived in our quaint little town and spent her days walking and praying over our community. That was what God had sent her to do, she said.

She stopped me that day and said, "I have to tell you this." Not knowing anything about my struggles, she spoke these words to me. "Sister, you don't listen to those voices; you listen to your daddy." I knew they were words directly from the Lord, because they grabbed my emotions, pierced my soul, and spoke directly to my spirit. Her words and encouragement often gave me the strength I needed to go on, and I am so thankful for her.

One of the greatest men that would also encourage me during my time in seminary was none other than Oswald Chambers. His devotionals were encouraging, and not only incredibly convicting for me, but often pierced my very being. The entry for March 11 would be of particular encouragement to me, and I would refer to it often:

OBEDIENCE TO THE "HEAVENLY VISION"
"*I was not disobedient to the heavenly vision*" (Acts 26:19, [ESV]).

If we lose "*the heavenly vision*" God has given us, we alone are responsible—not God. We lose the vision because of our own lack of spiritual growth. If we do not apply our beliefs about God to the issues of everyday life, the vision God has given us will never be fulfilled. The only way to be obedient of "the heavenly vision" is to give our upmost for His highest—our best for His glory. This can be accomplished only when we make a determination to continually remember God's vision. But the acid test is obedience to the vision in the details of our everyday life—sixty seconds out of every minute, and sixty minutes out of every hour, not just during times of personal prayer or public meetings.

"*Though it tarries, wait for it*" (Habakkuk 2:3, [NASB]). We cannot bring the vision to fulfillment through our own efforts, but must live under its inspiration until it fulfills itself. We try to be so practical that we forget the vision. At the very beginning we saw the vision but did not wait for it. We rushed off to do our practical work, and once the vision was fulfilled we could no longer even see it. Waiting for a vision that "tarries" is the true test of our faithfulness to God. It is at the risk of our own soul's welfare that we get caught up in practical busy-work, only to miss the fulfillment of the vision.

Watch for the storms of God. The only way God plants His saints is through the whirlwind of His storms. Will you be proven to be an empty pod with no seed inside? That will depend on whether or not you are actually living in the light of the vision you have seen. Let God send you out through His storm, and don't go until He does. If you select your own spot to be planted, you will prove yourself to be an unproductive, empty pod. However, if you allow God to plant you, you will "*bear much fruit*" (John 15:8).

It is essential that we live and "*walk in the light*" of God's vision for us (1 John 1:7).[2]

***

In my last year of seminary—on February 14, 2008, to be exact—two and a half months before my graduation, I was called into a meeting with some of the seminary professors. It seemed like it was an important meeting, yet once I arrived, I was confused that my program director wasn't present. In this meeting, I was informed that I wasn't going to be allowed to graduate in April. There were no reasons given, except that they felt that I was spiritually immature.

My grades were above acceptable, my course load was being kept up, and I had fulfilled all the requirements that they had laid out before me … but here I sat, broken, discouraged, confused, hurt, weeping, in this room with men who seemed to have hearts of stone, insisting that their only reason was that the seminary faculty thought I was too "spiritually immature."

---

[2] Oswald Chambers, *My Utmost for His Highest* (UK: Oswald Chambers Publications Association Ltd., 1992)

CHAPTER ELEVEN—SPREADING MY WINGS

They couldn't offer me any specific examples of what these conclusions were based on, nor would they offer me any explanation of their definition of "spiritually maturity," other than to say that the decision had been made and there was nothing I could do about it. They explained to me that I needed to find another spiritual mentor who could walk me through one year of spiritual growth, and then they would review my case in a year's time, and perhaps I could graduate in 2009.

Three years of pouring out my entire being into school, over ninety successful papers submitted, in addition to all of the reading, research, preparation, class time, and biblical study. Three hard years of abandoning everything else in my life, at times even my own children, so that a handful of men who thought I just wasn't cut out for their mold could have the final satisfaction of yanking the carpet out from under my feet in my last stretch of the race!

I walked out of that office that day so broken, feeling more alone and discouraged than I'd ever felt in all my time there. When I got home, my best friend was waiting for me to see how my meeting went and what it was all about. Two steps into the door, I collapsed to my knees, weeping from the very core of my being. I had reached the point of sheer exhaustion from the deeply-seated grief and what seemed to be relentless attacks on my life.

The professor in charge of my program could not discuss the matter, and offered me no consolation, which was very out of character considering the relationship we'd developed over the last three years. It was almost like he was detaching himself, because this was out of his control. All he said was, "Bonnie, I fought for you, but there is nothing I can do at this point. It's out of my hands." I often wonder how difficult that time was for him too. He had invested so much time, energy, and belief in me to push me through, to get me to the end.

Something told me that there was a much larger scene happening here, behind closed doors, that I knew very little about, nor would I ever be privy to. But what this room full of male Christian leaders forgot to anticipate when they took it upon themselves to make decisions on my behalf, was that it was me they were dealing with. To their disadvantage, they had severely underestimated the tenacious spirit that God had given me. They also seemed so blinded by their own religious pride, that they couldn't see that I had the Lord's favour. The very fact that I had made it this far was outstanding proof of that!

When I got home that day, I got down on my knees and sought the Lord in my room. He told me to come away and spend time with Him in the mountains. Friends of mine told me just to go and not worry one minute about the kids, so I got in my little car and drove west, weeping for the entire duration of the drive. In those next few days that I would spend broken before the Lord, in communion with Him alone, He would not only console me and comfort me, but He would show me how to handle this situation.

I came home from that weekend and made an appointment with the President of the College and Seminary. He explained to me the process of what I would need to do, should I decide to appeal their decision, though he warned me—not to discourage me, but to help me grasp the reality of the situation—that he didn't know of anyone who had ever won their appeal.

I had two weeks to write my appeal paper. I stated my case as unemotionally as I possibly could, poking holes in their decision with questions such as, "Why, if this was the feeling of the seminary faculty, did nobody come alongside me to help mentor me spiritually, to help me grow and learn? After all, this is why I was here."

I plainly stated my case that I had fulfilled all of the requirements that had been laid out before me for graduation, and here it was, only two and a half months before graduation, and this was the first I was hearing about their combined feelings of my "spiritual maturity," or lack thereof, and, more importantly, that those feelings would prevent me from graduating!

During the weeks that I awaited a response from the appeal board, it seemed liked an eternity! I tried to focus and continue in the work, in the event that I would win my appeal. I still had papers due, including the big one.

On March 15, 2008, I got my answer. I won my appeal and I would be graduating! I was beyond elated! Even though walking the hallways of the seminary would prove to be very difficult during those last few weeks, and I still had to endure my exit interviews, I knew that God was on my side, and that is all I needed!

On April 22, 2008, after three long years of perseverance through seminary, I wrote this in my journal: "I feel like I have lost my passion. I truly feel like I've been beaten up and my love, strength, fire, and passion are gone. Help me, Lord." I desperately needed help in those last few weeks. I needed His help to get to the finish line!

On April 26, at my graduation, I was hooded. Even though there were hundreds in that auditorium, it was a moment that I shared with God alone as I felt His Holy Spirit come upon me. After all, it was He who had given me the strength to persevere. It was from Him that I learned the most. It was Him that I wanted to please.

After he hooded me, the professor in charge of my program gave me a big hug and said, "Well, you did it, girl!" I knew he was bursting with pride. I walked across that stage in front of the college and seminary faculty, knowing that they all knew my trials of the past few months.

I wondered for a moment, as I walked in front of them, just how many of them were against me. It didn't matter anymore, as I knew that God was for me! It was time for me to spread my wings! I held my head high, turned, and smiled at all of them as I walked across that stage to accept my Masters degree from our president, who was grinning from ear to ear!

Chapter Twelve

BRIDLED

In the Bible, Habakkuk was a prophet who suffered many trials. One of the greatest lessons that Habakkuk would eventually learn was that during each of his trials, including when he didn't understand, he had been under God's sovereignty all along. The trials were for his own benefit, for his "pruning," and for God's purposes and glory.

This changed Habakkuk, and he would come to trust that God would bring about justice as He saw fit, and that He always sees the best way, even when we don't. In this, Habakkuk found great joy, even in hard circumstances, because He was able to fully trust that God had a plan and knew what He was doing.

Like Habakkuk, my life was dramatically changed once God gave me this new perspective. Many of the choices that I made in my life were made out of my own hurt, anger, and selfishness. Many of the hard times that I endured, that my children endured, and that the people around me endured, were because of my choices, my sin, and my brokenness. But once God revealed Himself to me, once I acknowledged His presence in my life, once I was able to put the pain and pride behind me and get real with Him and come to Him, broken and on my knees in repentance, He was able to show me His hand in all of my sufferings. Even though I'd made a lot of poor choices, He had allowed them and was able to use them for my benefit.

He was able to show me how to be thankful for my trials, because they have made me the woman of God that I am today. They have each been for my "pruning," for the building of my character and my faith. Like Habakkuk, I have found great joy in this, no matter what circumstances, whether trial or blessing. I have come to find joy and gratitude in it all. This is the gift of faith, and it is only from the Lord.

I would come to realize that even though my years in seminary were the most difficult years of my life, that is exactly the way the Lord intended it. Many tears, much transformation, and numerous trials had to take place in order for Him to prepare me for the calling He would place on my life once seminary was complete.

If an athlete wants to become a good athlete, he or she must endure hard training. Their trainer would be doing them no favour to send them into a world of tough competition if they hadn't prepared them completely. It's kind of like Mr. Miagi in *Karate Kid*. Even though "the kid" didn't understand or see the value in some of the seemingly meaningless tasks Mr. Miagi asked of him, and there were times when he didn't understand the harsh treatment, Mr. Miagi knew all along what he was preparing "the kid" for. He knew what "the kid" would have to endure to be ready.

Though I didn't see the full picture then, I see my "training" in seminary as favour from the Lord, and I am humbled and so thankful for it.

***

I believe that one of the hardest things we do in life is to be in relationship with one another, no matter what kind of relationship it is. I believe that the secret to relationships is forgiveness, and the secret to forgiveness is prayer, and the secret to prayer is humility.

> I believe that the secret to relationships is forgiveness, and the secret to forgiveness is prayer, and the secret to prayer is humility.

Sometimes people in your life do things, or continue to do things that make forgiveness really hard. Sometimes things happen in your life and you can't even imagine offering forgiveness. Forgiveness is not forgetting, excusing, or even allowing; forgiving means "to give up claim on, to cease to feel resentment." That takes humility. No matter how much you feel entitled to live in your anger and bitterness, the person who is most affected by your forgiveness, or lack of, towards others, is not them—it is you. Unforgiveness is poison to your spirit, your soul, and your body. It is like toxic waste that seeps in slowly, infiltrating your every emotion, your every thought, your entire being, until it slowly and steadily destroys you, everyone, and everything around you, unless you choose to stop it. But when you choose, in humility, to forgive, it begins an unending cycle of healing, reconciliation, and agape love. It grows in you a pure desire to see the best for each other.

Forgiveness can restore our broken world, one person at a time. But this is key: true forgiveness is not possible unless you are living and abiding in the love and grace of this man we call Jesus. It is only through our heartfelt humility and repentance to God, our Father, and through the sacrificial blood of His Son, Jesus Christ, that He is able to offer us this gift of His grace and forgiveness freely, without condition. Unless you have received the gift yourself, you cannot possibly give the gift as freely as it has been given to you. I can forgive only because I am "forgiven." Forgiveness brings out the nature of the light and love of Jesus in your life. "*A new command I give you: Love one another. As I have loved you, so you must love one another*" (John 13:34, NIV).

These are the words of Jesus himself, and it is the only answer for the sorry state of our world today. It is only through Him that any of this is possible. It's through identifying ourselves with the light and love of Jesus that the power of the Holy Spirit can transform our hearts and our lives. I know and have experienced this first-hand! Trust me when I say that Jesus is the only way home. You will get lost any other way!

***

The path of the journey of life is different for each one of us. This is the beauty of life; we have each been given this gift. To be honest, my path didn't become easier when I decided to live my life for God's purposes rather than my own, but it did become complete … because I had finally fulfilled my greatest need and became reconciled to my Father.

The most profound lesson that I have learned in life is this: life is about a relationship with God. This is our only purpose in life. It's not about the things we gain, our success in life, or even religion. It's about a one to one relationship with your Heavenly Father, where you learn to let Him walk you through life.

There is a purpose and a lesson in every person and every experience that comes into our life, and they aren't all going to be easy ones. But if we can learn to let God have our reins, He will be surefooted for us.

***

My story would not be complete without sharing with you this most valuable part. I believe that once I allowed God to fill the voids in me that needed filling, and gave Him the authority in my life, it was then that His grace readied me for the gift of love from a godly man, and that is when I met my husband, Bruce Rawling.

The day we met was divinely appointed, and our friendship was divinely blessed. God had sent me a best friend who would help me walk through some of the these most difficult trials, and I would help him walk through his own very difficult and painful trials. We were a gift to each other, and we are so thankful that God is a God of second chances and new beginnings. We were married on August 8, 2008 (08/08/08), because 8 is the number of "new beginnings" in the Bible. He is my best friend, a patient and servant-hearted husband, the godly man of our house, and an incredible father to our children.

Bruce and I have come to learn that no matter what trials bring difficulty to us, nothing can shake the foundation of our marriage or our faith, which is rooted in Jesus Christ. In each other, we have found a new beginning, a new hope, deep healing, wholeness, forgiveness, love, and an unwavering abandoned faith together. We have learned that with God at the helm, we can trust wherever He is leading, as long as we "stay the course."

***

CHAPTER TWELVE—BRIDLED

A wild mustang runs aimlessly through the wilderness ... through bushes, trees, and dangers. Occasionally it steps in a hole and gets injured because it has been careless, undisciplined, and unlearned. Dealing with the harshness of its habitat, it's left alone to survive.

I have spent much of my life running like a wild mustang—lost, unbridled, and undisciplined. I've run aimlessly through the harshness of life, feeling afraid and often alone. And then God got a hold of my life, showed Himself to me, and gave me a taste of His love, grace, forgiveness, and mercy.

Like a trainer gently works with a horse until the horse is ready to "join up" with him, God patiently did the groundwork with me until I was ready to allow Him to "bridle me in" and bring me into the purposes that He had for my life. A broken, bridled, submissive, and obedient horse is one of the greatest blessings that a horse-master could ever have in his life. I want to be this for our Lord Jesus Christ, my Master. No more shall I be unbridled.

Epilogue

Remember the "woman at the well" I mentioned at the beginning of this book? When Jesus met her there, it was with gentleness and compassion that He told her about everything she had ever done, all of her sin, yet He still loved her. He revealed to her His love, grace, and forgiveness. He gave her hope. When Jesus was with her, He asked her for a drink from the well, and then He told her about the living water that she could have. She would never thirst again if she would just drink of the living water. That living water is Him.

Let me tell you why I share my story with you. It's not to gather a choir of sympathy, or put any other person in a bad light. It's for this simple reason: to authentically share with you a message of repentance and forgiveness through grace and hope in Jesus Christ, the author of my life and your life, our redeemer, and our only hope for the "healing of the nations" (Revelation 22:2).

I have made many mistakes in my life, and many of those have caused hurt. I have played my part in many of the stories that I talk about when I share "my story." For a very long time, I lived my life in way that acted out my hurt, living entrenched in anger and selfishness. But like the woman at the well, I am forgiven.

Bruce's song: "Thirsty"

***

Everyone has a story. My story is just one, but it is mine. Remember that person that I asked you to think about at the beginning of the book? They too have a story, and it's one that you probably don't know. Everyone who plays a part in "my story" has his or her own story too, one that I probably don't know. My cousin who sexually molested me has his own story that I don't know. Each one of the men that played a part in my life has a story. Each person who played a part in my seminary experiences has their own story. Who am I to judge and say that anyone doesn't deserve forgiveness and a fresh start?

If I have been given this gift after all I have done, why shouldn't they deserve the same? Does this mean that I want to be in close relationship with any of them? No. To be honest, I do not. But it does mean that I can pray from a pure heart that they would accept the same gift from God that He has given me—His grace and His forgiveness.

My world was a hurting world. This world is a hurting world. It's time for us to just get real and honest with each other. We go about life trying to fill our needs, trying to be something we're not, so we can seem like we have something we don't. We lie, cheat, cover up, hide, pretend, boast, brag, and act like we have it all together, as though we're better than our neighbour. Our goals in life are big houses, fancy cars, successful jobs, and stuff … more and more stuff. Because the more we have, the more it appears that we're okay, and the less we look like we "need." We keep ourselves distracted so that we don't have to face reality, but the truth is that most of us are really hurting.

If we aren't hurting from things that have happened to us, things we have experienced or our own choices, we're hurting from things we've done to hurt others. Martin Luther believed, and I have to agree, that we are hurting from being slaves to our own selfishness.

I believe that we are hurting because we have divorced ourselves from our true Father, our greatest need. Our world is diseased; like a leprous area of skin that grows and infects more of the surrounding body, our selfishness, greed, lust, complete lack of repentance, and lack of love and respect for our fellow brothers and sisters infects our world, and the plague is too catastrophic to sustain us without divine intervention. It's time for us to get real! It's time for us to realize our "need" for Jesus. I tell you the truth ... He lives! And I, for one, desperately need Him in my life!

Bruce's song: "Need"

About the Author

First and foremost, I am a daughter and princess of the King Most High. I am so thankful that Jesus saved me and has forgiven me! I seek to live my life in humility before the Lord, being ever teachable, in obedience to Him, shining my light for Jesus every day of my life, and living out the will and purpose that He has for my life.

Secondly, I am an abundantly blessed wife. In my opinion, Bruce Rawling is the most patient, gentle, humble, and pure-in-heart man that God has ever created. He is my best friend, confidant, and faith partner, patiently accepting my rough edges and sometimes harsh nature, and loving me through my faults to find the core of who I truly am in Christ. I am so thankful for the gift of grace and second chances that God gave us when He brought us together.

Thirdly, I am a mother of three amazingly beautiful young women! I have spent my entire life intentionally pouring myself out for my children and putting them first in all things. Though I have certainly made many mistakes, I have done my best to discern and meet their emotional, mental, physical, and spiritual needs. I have raised my girls to be strong, independent, fierce young women for the Lord. I have raised them to fly.

Lastly, along with many lessons from the school of "hard knocks," I also have a versatile educational background in Social Work, Primary Care Paramedic, Power Engineering, and Youth and Family Ministry (MA). Yet the most important thing that I have learned in my life is that none of those accomplishments or awards matter in the end. My only goal and purpose in life is to be in such a close relationship with my Heavenly Father, through the Holy Spirit, that I am seeking and obeying His will every day.

My life is a gift from Him; in fact, I believe He gave me life twice, and I choose to pour it out every day back to Him. If I ever lose sight of this sole purpose for my life, I will consider my life unsuccessful.

My prayer for each person reading this book is that in some way you will be encouraged, strengthened, educated, built up, or spurred on to intentionally seek God's will and purpose for your own life! Every person is put on this earth for a special purpose that only YOU can fulfill! Never, never, never give up until you find out what that purpose is … and then fulfill it!

"I can do all things through Christ who strengthens me" (Philippians 4:13).

All my love and encouragement,
Bonnie Rawling

Other Books

In 2012, the Lord told Bruce and Bonnie Rawling to sell everything and come follow Him. They did just that! Selling their 3,500 sq. ft., five-bedroom home and acreage, they downsized to a tour bus and spent the next three years on the road, following wherever God told them to go. They founded a non-profit organization called Tree of Life—Hope Foundation, which, following the leading of the Holy Spirit, became their life and ministry. You can learn about their ministry at: www.treeoflife.hope@live.com.

In her first book, *Forgiven*, Bonnie shares the story of her life—the betrayal, abuse, pain, and ultimate healing she experienced through the power of the Holy Spirit. In a straightforward and riveting voice, she leads readers into the darkest hour of her soul, and then lifts them into the realm of joy as the light of Christ shines into her life and gives her the grace to find freedom through forgiveness.

In her next book, *The Condition of Our Heart*, Bonnie shares their faith journey, the stretching times of discipline and refining fire from the Lord, as well as the many, many incredible miracle stories which testify that we serve a faithful, loving, and living God!